xx

Zapata
Dallas, 12.I.1991

NUMBER SEVENTEEN

The Walter Prescott Webb Memorial Lectures

Essays on the Family
and Historical Change

[THE WALTER PRESCOTT WEBB MEMORIAL LECTURES]

Essays on the Family and Historical Change

BY DAVID LEVINE, LESLIE PAGE MOCH,

LOUISE A. TILLY, JOHN MODELL,

ELIZABETH PLECK

Introduction by LESLIE PAGE MOCH

Edited by LESLIE PAGE MOCH

and GARY D. STARK

Published for the University of Texas at Arlington by
Texas A & M University Press: College Station

Library of Congress Cataloging in Publication Data
Main entry under title:

Essays on the family and historical change.

(The Walter Prescott Webb memorial lectures; 17)
Contents: Proto-Industrialization and demographic upheaval / David Levine—
Infirmities of the body and vices of the soul / Leslie Page Moch—Rich and poor in a
French textile city / Louise A. Tilly—[etc.]
1. Family—United States—History—Addresses, essays, lectures. 2. Family—Eu-
rope—History—Addresses, essays, lectures. 3. United States—Economic conditions—
Addresses, essays, lectures. 4. Europe—Economic conditions—Addresses, essays, lec-
tures. 5. United States—Social conditions—Addresses, essays, lectures. 6. Europe—
Social conditions—Addresses, essays, lectures. I. Levine, David, 1946- . II. Moch,
Leslie Page. III. Stark, Gary D., 1948- . IV. Series.
HQ535.E77 1983   306.8'5'0973   82-45900
ISBN 0-89096-151-4

Manufactured in the United States of America
FIRST EDITION

Contents

Introduction
    Leslie Page Moch   3

Proto-Industrialization and Demographic Upheaval
    David Levine   9

Infirmities of the Body and Vices of the Soul: Migrants, Family,
and Urban Life in Turn-of-the-Century France
    Leslie Page Moch   35

Rich and Poor in a French Textile City
    Louise A. Tilly   65

Dating Becomes the Way of American Youth
    John Modell   91

The Whipping Post for Wife Beaters, 1876–1906
    Elizabeth Pleck   127

Contributors   151

Essays on the Family
and Historical Change

Introduction

ON March 12, 1982, the University of Texas at Arlington sponsored the Seventeenth Annual Walter Prescott Webb Memorial Lectures. The four lectures delivered this year, as well as the winning entry in the Webb-Smith essay competition, explore the interaction between the family and historical change in the United States and Europe.

In recent years, increasing numbers of scholars have used the family as a prism through which to view historical change.[1] Why is this so? What does a familial perspective yield that is lacking in a focus on individuals or larger social groups? The decisions, values, and choices made in the family arena provide the most information about the life circumstances of historical actors because the family was long the basic unit of production and remains an important unit of consumption. The social support and working hands of family members were the only resources most people could mobilize, and as a result the family was often the sole mediator of changing circumstances.[2] The ways in which people coped with their world, then, were most immediately reflected in familial decisions. Consequently, a focus on the family has allowed historians the clearest view of the dynamic relationship between the people of the past and the evolution of society and economy.

An example from one wellspring of family history, historical demography, illustrates how a focus on familial matters uncovers the dialectic between actor and circumstance: Louis Henry, pioneer scholar in the discipline, reconstituted family histories from parish records in order to investigate natural fertility—that is, reproductive patterns of the traditional world—before industrialization and urbanization pre-

---

[1] For information about the development of family history, see two recent review articles: Lawrence Stone, "Family History in the 1980s," *Journal of Interdisciplinary History* 12, no. 1 (Summer, 1981): 51–87, and Louise A. Tilly and Miriam Cohen, "Does the Family Have a History?" *Social Science History* 6, no. 2 (Spring, 1982): 131–79.

[2] For a full explanation of this perspective, see Louise A. Tilly and Joan W. Scott, *Women, Work and Family* (New York: Holt, Rinehart and Winston, 1978).

sumably inspired birth control and the rational calculation that was thought to accompany such changes. Henry, like many succeeding demographers, found that natural fertility was a chimera.[3] Rather, the number of children born to the family of the past was influenced by the social and economic context in which marriage and conception occurred. This insight into variations in marriage and childbirth provided the first crack in a long-held idea that traditional society was immobile. That notion "shattered on contact with the last few decades' research on European social and economic history."[4]

Family history grew in part from interest in patterns of birth, death, and marriage in the past, but it has become a revealing arena for inquiries into the evolution of the economy, sentiments, sexuality, the role of women, life stages, household structure, and systems of lineage and kin. In the course of the last decade, some basic questions have been answered. We now know, for example, the fundamental forms and fluctuations in the organization of the family. The shape of the decline of birth and death rates in the West over the past two hundred years has been described by the Princeton Office of Population Studies. The current primary avenues of inquiry investigate demographic patterns, household economics, and sentiments, and scholars are responding to the call to explore new areas such as the neglected relationships between politics, women's power, and the family.[5] As one scholar observed, "Family history is now inextricably bound up with all of the major debates over historical sources, methods, problems, and interpretations."[6] One important disagreement centers on sentiments and values: historians of the family disagree on their ability to assess the emotional climate of family life, how it has changed, or even its importance to our understanding of the family.[7]

[3] Louis Henry, *Anciennes familles genevoises* (Paris: Institut National des Etudes Démographiques, 1956); Henry and E. Gautier, *La Population de Crulai* (Paris: Institut National des Etudes Démographiques, 1958).

[4] Charles Tilly, "Flows of Capital and Forms of Industry in Europe, 1500–1900" (Working Paper No. 263, Center for Research on Social Organization, University of Michigan), pp. 16–17.

[5] See Tilly and Cohen, "Does the Family Have a History?"

[6] Stone, "Family History in the 1980s," p. 86.

[7] See, for example, the contrast between the assessments of Stone, "Family History in the 1980s," pp. 82–83, and those of Tilly and Cohen, "Does the Family Have a History?" pp. 142–46, of the future of this line of inquiry. See also Charles Tilly and Louise Tilly, "Stalking the Bourgeois Family," *Social Science History* 4, no. 2 (Spring, 1980): 251–60.

Because the basic shape of the family over the past five hundred years has been described, although often without sufficient care in linking evidence and argument, many historians are turning from the large tomes and overarching descriptions of the evolution of the family to local studies, systematic comparisons, and more careful use of evidence.[8] In so doing, family studies are being enriched by the sensitivities, sources, and methods of other fields, notably anthropology, demography, economics, and sociology. This is fitting because the family clearly is a demographic and economic unit as well as a social one. Like the best of history in any area, the most valuable family studies today address large questions that are meaningful to all historians and useful to a broader understanding of large-scale change.

This volume offers five essays that are of general interest because although they properly focus on well-defined questions and specific locales, each evokes a broader question. Together they expand our understanding of the family as a mediator of economic change and a telling locus for values. Each combines sources and questions that push the inquiry beyond the confines of a single perspective. By crossing the border between an understanding of the working-class family, rooted in an economic perspective (based on demographic and census data), and the middle class and elite family, rooted in an anthropological perspective (based on literary evidence), these essays move toward correcting a major deficiency in family history: the mutually exclusive nature of inquiries into upper- and lower-class family life. Both economics and cultural values affect familial behavior, according to all five authors, but the perspectives, sources, and specific problems posed by each give this collection considerable breadth.

In his essay "Proto-Industrialization and Demographic Upheaval," David Levine investigates the dynamic relationship between economic change and family—the linchpin to our understanding of demographic change. Levine, whose essay won the Webb-Smith competition, focuses on historical processes whose importance has been highlighted only in the last decade: proto-industrialization, deindustrialization, and proletarianization. Here Levine is following up his pioneering re-

---

[8] Investigations spanning centuries include Philippe Ariès, *Centuries of Childhood: A Social History of Family Life* (New York: Knopf, 1962); Lloyd De Mause, ed., *The History of Childhood* (New York: Psychohistory Press, 1974); Edward Shorter, *The Making of the Modern Family* (New York: Basic Books, 1975); and Lawrence Stone, *The Family, Sex, and Marriage in England, 1500–1800* (New York: Harper and Row, 1977).

search, which showed how cottage industry was instrumental in pro-
letarianizing the family by hastening its dependence on wage labor and
thus releasing it from constraints on family formation and fertility.[9] He
uses the demographer's classic technique of family reconstitution to investigate two English communities: nineteenth-century Shepshed in
Leicestershire and seventeenth-century Colyton in Devonshire. To
this technique he adds an analysis of how families responded to deindustrialization and depression. The proto-industrial family, Levine
concludes, responded to this economic development with a strategy of
early marriage and high fertility; these same demographic decisions
also exacerbated the families' subsequent hardship.

My essay, "Infirmities of the Body and Vices of the Soul: Migrants,
Family, and Urban Life in Turn-of-the-Century France," is related to
Levine's insofar as it, too, attempts to link changes in population patterns to the economy. In this case, the demographic process is migration to the city, and particular urban areas shape the economic environment. What kinds of urban economies encouraged the migration
of families together? What kinds attracted young, single migrants?
These questions are posed of the cities receiving a massive influx of
newcomers in urbanizing Europe. My evidence is of two distinct types:
on the one hand, contemporary observations by reformers and urban
histories; on the other, a systematic comparison of population patterns
from the census lists of Amiens, Nîmes, and Roubaix, France. I conclude that although family connections were related to migration to the
city, only the factory city, by its employment patterns, was able to promote family migration because it provided jobs for several family
members simultaneously. In this essay, migrants' language and religious culture are seen as factors that can facilitate migrants' integration
into urban society or can encourage them to maintain a separate
identity.

Louise Tilly also explores the urban family in the centerpiece essay
"Rich and Poor in a French Textile City." Like the two previous essays,
it is grounded in an understanding of the family as a key unit in economic decision making.[10] Tilly goes beyond the perspective of house-

[9] David Levine, *Family Formation in an Age of Nascent Capitalism* (New York: Academic Press, 1977).

[10] Tilly and Scott, *Women, Work and Family*; Louise A. Tilly, "Individual Lives and
Family Strategies in the French Proletariat," *Journal of Family History* 4 (Summer,
1979): 137–52.

hold economics and the working-class family by combining the observations of contemporary ethnographers and studies of the local bourgeoisie with urban census data. She investigates the family strategies of the factory workers and the bourgeoisie of Roubaix, France, and in so doing places evidence about attitudes, aspirations, and values face-to-face with evidence about the family economy. Tilly demonstrates how workers' familial concerns were reflected in their protest, an arena of inquiry neglected by family historians. Bourgeois and worker families alike, she concludes, controlled their members to the benefit of the group, but the areas of control of each were unique to them.

John Modell traces the development of an escape from family control, the date, in "Dating Becomes the Way of American Youth." As the dating system spread, it developed and articulated norms that were to influence the lives of individual adolescents and American culture between the 1930s and 1970s. As an investigation into the life stage of adolescence, Modell's essay is part of a growing branch of family history that focuses on the evolution of various stages of the life cycle.[11] These studies offer subtlety and flexibility by intersecting the life course of the individual with family and historical change. Modell's essay is exemplary, combining wide sources of change with a close investigation of a social phenomenon. It focuses on the sentiments and values that created the implicit rules for dating in the context of the 1920s, a period when increased leisure and income and the growth of age-graded high schools made it possible for dating to develop. Evidence of adolescents' values comes from such sources as popular magazines and teens' letters to their high school newspapers. Consequently, Modell offers a clear link between values and behavior, thus overcoming a weakness in the studies of sentiments and the family.

Likewise, Elizabeth Pleck inquires into the impact of particular values in "The Whipping Post for Wife Beaters, 1876–1906." This essay refines the question of the family with a focus on the desire to ma-

---

[11] See Glen Elder, "Family History and the Life Course," in *Transitions: The Family and the Life Course in Historical Perspective*, ed. Tamara Hareven (New York: Academic Press, 1978), pp. 17–64. This essay is part of a larger study of the evolution of the life cycle in America; see John Modell, "Normative Aspects of Marriage Timing since World War II," *Journal of Family History* 5 (Summer, 1980): 210–34; John Modell, Frank Furstenberg, and Theodore Hershberg, "Social Change and Transitions to Adulthood," in *Philadelphia: Work, Space, Family and Group Experience in a Nineteenth Century City*, ed. T. Hershberg (New York: Oxford University Press, 1981), pp. 311–41.

nipulate familial behavior by public policy; it investigates both the impetus behind a national movement in the United States to punish wife beaters and the ideology of the movement's leaders.[12] By investigating the values behind an elite's concern with battered women, Pleck uncovers not only pity for defenseless women, but racism and nativism as well. In this instance the intersection of values with economic and social power is clear, because we see class and race play an important role in policy questions regarding the family. Pleck's essay rests on records of the legal profession, sources that family historians have only begun to tap.

Drawing evidence from a variety of sources—parish records, census lists, ethnographers' reports, court trial records, and the complaints of socially ostracized adolescents—these five essays enrich our understanding of family members as a locus of public concern and private decisions. We see the family responding to economic changes brought on by the growth of cottage industry, by a move to the city, and by times of depression. We see how the family unit managed its members in very different economic circumstances and thereby see its values articulated through its decisions. A study of high schoolers shows how norms change in concert with circumstance. In the last essay included here, we see those with wealth and power wield their resources to evaluate and condemn the behavior of the poor. Together these five essays combine the economics and values of the family, two elements whose separation has been an impediment to our best understanding of its history.

The editors of this volume wish to express their gratitude to the authors of these essays, the audience of the lecture series, the faculty of the University of Texas at Arlington, and C. B. Smith, whose esteem for Walter Prescott Webb inspired this lecture series and whose generous support makes it possible.

[12] See also Elizabeth Pleck, "Wife Beating in Nineteenth Century America," *Victimology* 4, no. 1 (1979): 60–74.

DAVID LEVINE

Proto-Industrialization and Demographic Upheaval

PROTO-INDUSTRIALIZATION and demographic upheaval—such a formulation seems to beg two questions that will be addressed in my presentation. First, How did proto-industry, or cottage industry, cast asunder traditional social arrangements maintaining a form of demographic equilibrium or homeostasis? and second, What was the impact of depression and *deindustrialization* on the family strategies of a proletarianized rural industrial population? After some general introductory remarks that will provide a schematic outline of the opportunities for household formulation by referring to a number of English family reconstitution studies, I will focus the discussion on two particular cases: Shepshed, Leicestershire, in the early nineteenth century and Colyton, Devonshire, in the seventeenth century.[1] In the concluding section the insights gained from these two village studies will be related to the broader themes of economic change, proletarianization, and family life during the first Industrial Revolution.

My previous work tried to show that population growth in the early industrial period was dependent upon contemporaneous changes in the structure of English society. It was my central concern to describe how the transformation of peasants and artisans into agricultural and industrial proletarians resulted in the estrangement of growing sections of the population from the sociodemographic controls that had previously maintained a balance between population and resources. The interplay between economic and demographic change was examined in the light of information derived from four family reconstitution studies, of Shepshed and Bottesford in Leicestershire; Terling, Essex; and Colyton, Devon. These communities were chosen because they

[1] A fuller account of the demographic history of these two villages can be found in my monograph *Family Formation in an Age of Nascent Capitalism* (New York: Academic Press, 1977).

fulfilled the necessary prerequisites of having fairly detailed and comprehensive parish registers while being economically quite distinct. Shepshed, an unregulated freehold village on the edge of Charnwood Forest, was the most intensively proto-industrialized community in Leicestershire. In contrast, Bottesford was a purely agricultural village that was dominated—physically, socially, and economically—by the Dukes of Rutland. The framework knitting industry was successfully kept off the Rutlands' estate in the belief that "the connection between industry and poverty . . . was simple and direct." Terling, in the rolling hills of central Essex, had experienced the switch to capitalist farming early—by the seventeenth century. Its precocious modernity was reflected in the early appearance of the tripartite rural social formation—landlord, tenant farmers, and wage laborers. Colyton, in eastern Devon, was the first English village population to be reconstituted. E. A. Wrigley's pioneering work on Colyton is so well known and frequently quoted that it proved to be the perfect choice for inclusion in my revisionist study.[2] Moreover, the fact that Wrigley only tangentially related demographic behavior to economic change proved to be reason to reconsider this particular study further. And last, the fact that the hard grind of reconstituting the village population was already completed played no small part in helping me to choose Colyton.

Evidence derived from the four family reconstitution studies showed that the availability of employment, whether in industry or agriculture, had important implications for determining at what age to marry. When employment became available to all who were willing to sell their labor, it was no longer possible to maintain the equilibrating mechanism of late marriage: men (and women) could reach their maximum earning capacity at an early age, and there was, therefore, no rea-

---

[2] E. A. Wrigley, "Mortality in Pre-industrial England: The Example of Colyton, Devon Over Three Centuries," *Daedulus* 97 (1968): 546–80, and idem, "Family Limitation in Pre-industrial England," in *Population in Industrialization*, ed. M. Drake (London: Methuen, 1969), pp. 157–94. Family reconstitution was first employed on French material by Louis Henry, who devised the technique. E. A. Wrigley's work on Colyton demonstrated its value to English scholars. Family reconstitution is a beguilingly simple technique. One treats a parish register rather like a giant jigsaw puzzle, the pieces being the particles of information describing individual demographic events (i.e., births, deaths, and marriages). One arranges this material into families of origin ("demographic units of production") through a long and laborious but relatively straightforward process of selection and organization. Once this manual work is completed it becomes possible to analyze the assembled data according to whatever criteria one wishes.

son to postpone marriage. A lower age at marriage resulted in a longer childbearing period with the effect that, in the absence of family limitations, the birth rate rose. Further evidence suggested that the argument linking population growth with the death rate is of only limited value. In explaining population growth in rural, agricultural villages like Bottesford and Terling, the argument received some support, but even in those communities the influence of a declining death rate was no more important than that of a rising birth rate. In areas of high population density like Shepshed that were becoming proportionately more important during the Industrial Revolution, the death rate rose: it was wholly as a result of its rising birth rate that this industrial population increased.

Of course, wage labor was not a new phenomenon. It was encountered on thirteenth-century manors, and sixteenth-century justices of the peace made it their business to assess wage rates. In such instances of simple wage labor the achievement of maximum earning power came early. A simple, unskilled farm laborer, for instance, was in his prime by the age of twenty at the latest. However, in traditional, pre-capitalist England such men did not marry until their later twenties, and it may very well be that a sizable fraction may never have married at all. The explanation for this phenomenon of late, postponed marriage is, I believe, to be found in the social solidarity of the village community. Individuals who transgressed its "moral economy" were subject to public humiliation, which served to affirm the ways in which an inward-looking, seemingly changeless society governed behavior and projected its normative precept.[3] The demographic importance of this traditional *mentalité* was that this moral economy played a strong role in asserting the primacy of group norms against individual action. In a society that equated social maturity with economic independence, that regarded laborers as being unfree, and that subjected laborers-*cum*-servants to patriarchal household discipline, the age at marriage for such men (and women) was kept high. It was only when a position in the village economy became vacant that marriage was considered. Through the use of formal and informal constraints like "charivaris," "rough music," or "skimmington rides" the village community enforced the strategies of family formation that they had themselves created

---

[3] See, in particular, E. P. Thompson, "'Rough Music': Le charivari anglais," *Annales, E. S. C.* 27, no. 2 (1972): 285–312.

to promote a form of stability, an optimization of the demographic-economic balance so far as the group was concerned.[4] Capitalist relations of production enlarged the proportion of proletarians. Just as the material foundations of the traditional economy were undermined by the advent of capitalism so too were the modes of behavior that were essential props of this system. Thereafter, the decision to marry could be made in response to individual needs, not communal expectations. In this way the advent of capitalism undermined the social controls that had previously buttressed a system of late marriage. Moreover, the advent of capitalism increased the proportion of the population that was proletarianized, and this compositional change further lowered the age at marriage because it meant that groups marrying early became proportionately more important. And last, the advent of capitalism as a system meant that for the village laborer the period of wage dependency stretched to encompass his whole life. For the rural underclass the institution of wage labor became a lifelong condition, not just a phase in the life cycle. In the capitalist political economy the need for patriarchal discipline waned, the institution of service passed away, and a new set of social norms took its place. Thus, the argument has stressed the dynamic demographic potential that was unleashed when the village laborer was no longer governed by the "prudential check" of late, postponed marriage.

The second quarter of the nineteenth century in Shepshed is of particular interest because the villagers were confronted with drastically changed circumstances for which their recently acquired demographic profile was most unsuitable. The framework stocking-knitting industry, on which a very large proportion of the villagers were dependent, entered a state of severe depression after 1815. Real wages fell by about 40 percent. Emigration was one popular response to these conditions, and many young people left the village to seek better prospects elsewhere. Those who stayed, however, were ill-equipped to reduce the number of children they would inevitably bring into the world. Evidence derived from the reconstitution study showed that

[4]For readers wishing detailed evidence describing the demographic experience of Shepshed and Colyton, please see my book *Family Formation in an Age of Nascent Capitalism*, chaps. 5 and 7. I have tried to keep the quantitative evidence under a tight rein in this paper, and it has been selected to explicate the larger, more general argument put forward here.

women who married after 1825 were deliberately restricting their fertility as they grew older. This reduction in fertility was sufficient to counteract the effect of a further one-year fall in the age of marriage that extended the childbearing period. But by itself this deliberate regulation of marital fertility produced little change in the rate of natural increases. The observed decline in the net rate of reproduction in the semiurbanized village was caused by the deterioration in living conditions, which was exacerbated by the falling real incomes of framework knitters. Children born after 1825 had a life expectation at birth that was six years less than those born in the previous cohort.[5]

By the time of the 1851 census it was apparent that the framework knitters had further responded to their adverse economic circumstances by making adjustments in their household structure. These proto-industrial workers were quite conscious of the disastrous consequences that could befall a family in which the number of dependents outstripped the family's much reduced earning powers. In contrast to the neighboring agricultural laborers and village craftsmen, the framework knitters not only had the largest number of working wives, but their children were also most likely to have been contributing to the family income from an early age. In very few of their households was there just one wage earner: it was quite common for three or more household members to have been employed in the hosiery trade. Their propensity to live with relatives and lodgers was another way in which the number of coresident wage earners was increased. Among the framework knitters, more than one household in eight headed by a married man contained another coresident family, but among the nonindustrial villagers, such sharing was unusual—just one in twenty such complex households existed. The framework knitters' preference for living in large domestic units was part of a concerted effort to protect themselves from their precarious economic situation.

The causal arrows did not merely fly in one direction: economic activity transformed demographic behavior, but there was an equal reciprocal action in the other direction as population growth influenced the structure of proto-industry. Not only were the workers re-

[5] Franklin Mendels has noted that the Belgian proto-industrialists' response to fluctuations in their income was "asymmetrical." He has not studied their fertility but only their nuptiality. See Franklin Mendels, "Industrialization and Population Pressure in Eighteenth Century Flanders" (Ph.D. dissertation, University of Wisconsin, 1970).

placing themselves at a very rapid rate, but any sustained period of prosperity occasioned the influx of new recruits into the industry. For this reason, labor costs were kept at a low level. Because labor was both cheap and plentiful there was little incentive to undertake capital investments in order to raise productivity. In effect, these factors resulted in a vicious circle that has been called industrial involution. Low wages meant that primitive techniques were most profitable; therefore, this low-level technology was labor intensive, and cheap labor was of critical importance.

By dint of emigration, fertility restriction, child labor, and coresidence, the proto-industrial workers of Shepshed created a system that enabled them to survive in a state of industrial involution. But survival merely intensified the pressures. The effect of living in a demographic hothouse was that the framework knitters were both educationally and physically stunted by the experience.

Why did these villagers continue to follow a high-pressure reproductive strategy? An answer to this question must, I think, be framed in terms of the peculiar demographic and economic conditions of industrial involution. Of prime importance, therefore, is the economics of the family life cycle. For the framework knitter there appears to have been an incentive to marry early and, in particular, to concentrate marital fertility into the early years of marriage. The nature of the labor process made it inefficient for a machine operative to work alone because he needed supplementary help at a number of stages in his work. To do everything by himself meant that this supplementary work had to be paid for in the currency of the stockinger's own labor. Such supplementary work could be performed cheaply by dependent members of the framework knitter's own family. Moreover, the alternative of working in a frameshop was notoriously unattractive due to the confiscatory nature of the charges that were demanded from the individual knitter. Thus there was a positive incentive to set up an independent, family unit of production at an early age. This factor was of no small importance in shaping the proto-industrialists' marital planning and may account for their persistently marrying at an early age in the face of deteriorating conditions.

Of more importance to the fertility strategy the framework knitters displayed was the fact that once one married, it was economically most sensible to hurry over the stage during which the dependency ratio within the family was most disadvantageous. These years were the first ones in a marriage when children contributed nothing to the productive process and, in addition to their cost of support, they distracted the wife as mother so that her contribution was reduced. Not surprisingly, in the analysis of household structure at the time of the 1851 census it was found that a substantial number of families with no children or just one small child were living in coresidential domestic units. The exigencies of domestic production were not confined to young families; rather, they extended to all married couples whose family labor input was below some optimum level. This condition seems to be one reason why as many as one family in nine headed by a man in his late thirties was still found to be living in shared accommodation. The domestic economies of the process of production also seems to explain the reason why there was a positive incentive to have children in the early years of marriage because the sooner one's offspring could contribute to the family economy by helping the parents with the simple, supplementary operations, the sooner the family could emerge from the state of semidependency that characterized the first years of marriage. Finally, the cost of having an additional child was not commensurate with having the previous one. That is to say, the cost of having another child created a marginal cost that was not equal to the cost of the previous child and so was less than the average cost.[6]

Beyond these short-term calculations another factor may be of some importance in explaining the rise in marital fertility that accompanied the onset of proto-industrialization in mid-eighteenth-century Shepshed. This factor is the consideration of security in old age. By having more children a kind of retirement fund or pension plan was being built. Since these domestic workers had nothing of value except their physical skills, their earnings would tend to decline as they reached later middle age. In the sense that their children would themselves create individual units of production the older generation would be provided for in their declining years. They could put themselves into their children's domestic production units at precisely the time when the dependency ratios of the younger generation's families would be most adverse. To summarize the argument, then, it appears that

[6]S. Ledermann, *Nouvelles tables-types de mortalité* (Paris: Presses Universitaires de France, 1969), pp. 90, 135.

the framework knitters' demographic-economic system had two thrusts: first, to get over the dependency "hump" in early marriage as quickly as possible, and second, to be sure that at least one child survived in order to provide for old age.

Within the parameters and exigencies of this demographic-economic system an explanation for the perpetuation of the villagers' high-pressure reproduction strategy can be developed. In making this argument two factors are of paramount importance: first, the serious rise in infant and child mortality after 1825, and second, the lower age of brides in the post-1825 cohort. These two factors are themselves intertwined, and their real significance will only become apparent in the course of the explanation. Bearing in mind that it was of the utmost importance for these people to be survived by at least one child, we see that the sudden rise in infant mortality meant that a reproductive calculus based on pre-1825 life expectation was less relevant in the worsening climate after that date. Over and above the necessity of getting over the fertility "hump," which itself fostered high fertility in the early years of marriage, the rise in mortality meant that at the presumed end of this stage, say after six or seven years, it was less likely that there would be a surviving child. Thus the dependency state was attenuated, not least because mortality among the first and, to a lesser extent, second children was above normal. So, even if the couple wanted to limit the overall number of children they had, it was necessary to make sure that their first children were safely out of the early years, during which the risk of death was so great.

A contradiction, therefore, developed because of the increased uncertainty of each child's survival and also because it would be a great hardship to repeat the whole dependency stage by expecting that any individual child would survive. The resolution to this contradiction was a maintenance of high fertility until at least one child was old enough to begin to contribute his or her labor to the family economy. It was only at this point that conscious fertility limitation could commence. Evidence supporting this interpretation showed that women marrying under twenty-five were actively controlling their fertility five years earlier than their contemporaries who married after thirty. Such young brides, moreover, were far more successful in limiting their fertility after thirty than were a similar set of women who married before 1825. For the younger women marrying after 1825, fertility restriction not only commenced earlier, but it was also far more effective. It was not, however, totally effective; therefore, these women continued to bear children, albeit at a reduced rate, even after they had ensured that kind of old-age security for themselves and their husbands that was such a strong factor in promoting their earlier high fertility rates.

The second factor contributing to the perpetuation of a high rate of reproduction, the lower age at first marriage for women married after 1825, seems to be a statistical artifact. There appears to be two causes for this phenomenon. First, the cohort groupings blur the fact that by the 1790s something like a consensus regarding the age at first marriage seems to have emerged in this proto-industrial community. It is apparent that for women and, to a somewhat lesser extent, for their husbands there was a basic stability in the age at first marriage after 1790. It would be less likely that these people would begin to marry later in response to deteriorating real wages than that they would try to restrict fertility and have a greater propensity to live in coresident households. While it may be obvious to anyone who looks at the group dynamics of population growth that these strategies were of only limited value, the view of the individual mid-nineteenth-century framework knitter and his wife would be quite different. They were trying to protect themselves from their precarious circumstances in the most obvious ways, and because the exigencies of their household demographic-economic system were intensified, the alternative of later marriage does not seem to have been a real one. Anyhow, even if a framework knitter did want to marry later, the initial unfavorable dependency ratio could not be avoided. It was built into the contract, as it were.

The second cause of this statistical double vision stems from the bunching of age at marriage in the post-1825 period. There was a major reduction in the number of (relatively) older women marrying. Both the interquartile range and the standard deviation measure the width of the distribution of marriage ages, and both of these measures grew smaller after 1825 as the distribution became more peaked. The fact that the upper quartile age of marriage was 1.3 years earlier and that of the lower quartile fell by just 0.5 years after 1825 underlines this phenomenon.

The argument that has been developed so far assumes that the evidence derived from the village reconstitution study can be used to explain the behavior of one section of villagers, the framework knitters. Although the proto-industrialists formed by far the largest element in the village's socioeconomic mix, it would be incorrect to infer a direct relationship. Ideally the way to have proceeded with the argument would have been by breaking the sample into occupational groups and then comparing and contrasting the variations in demographic behavior both between groups and within groups across time. But due to the relative sparseness of occupational information presented for much of the period I studied, this procedure was not possible. For the last period, after 1825, it was. Therefore, let us turn our attention to this material.

Because the primary reason for this further examination was to determine the extent to which the framework knitters' demographic behavior differed from that of the other members of the community, I decided to make a simple split in the data. Thus the evidence details the characteristics of the framework knitters and "the others"—the farmers, laborers, shoemakers, carpenters, millers, bakers, and so on. The proliferation of occupational groups meant that meaningful information could not have been presented for any group, except perhaps agricultural laborers. And even for the laborers the number of observations was disconcertingly small. So, for the sake of providing at least a straightforward comparison, a degree of sociological precision was sac-

TABLE 1. Age At First Marriage, by Occupation

Group	N	Mean	Standard Deviation	Lower Quartile	Median	Upper Quartile	Interquartile Range
Men							
Framework							
knitters	268	23.6	4.6	20.9	23.0	26.7	5.8
Others	123	24.9	5.1	21.9	24.2	28.3	6.4
All	391	24.1	4.8	21.2	23.3	27.0	5.8
Women							
Framework							
knitters	312	22.3	3.6	19.9	21.8	24.3	4.4
Others	167	23.5	5.1	20.2	22.6	25.8	5.6
All	479	22.6	4.6	20.1	22.1	24.7	4.6

TABLE 2. Age-specific Fertility, by Occupation

Occupational Group by Age	Years at Risk	Children Born	Rate/100
Framework knitters			
Under 25	714	290	406
25–29	705	242	343
30–34	561	156	278
35–39	374	81	217
40–44	199	24	121
45–49	88	2	23
Others			
Under 25	415	196	472
25–29	416	154	370
30–34	337	116	344
35–39	188	51	271
40–44	113	14	124
45–49	32	0	0
All			
Under 25	1,129	486	430
25–29	1,121	396	350
30–34	898	272	303
35–39	562	132	235
40–44	312	38	122
45–49	120	2	17

rificed. Furthermore, the reader should bear in mind that the lines of distinction between the framework knitters and the other members of the community are not as hard and fast as might be expected. Some of the laborers' wives and, to a lesser extent, the tradesmen's wives and craftsmen's wives were involved in the stocking trade as knitters or seamers.

The two groups' nuptiality (Table 1) and age-specific marital fertility (Table 2) show quite clearly that not only were the framework knitters' brides about one year younger than the brides of those in other occupational groups, but that they had a significantly lower level of fertility throughout the most fecund years of their childbearing period.

Occupationally undifferentiated results from the family reconstitu-

TABLE 3. Fertility Restriction by Age at Marriage, by Occupation

Occupational Group	Under 25	25–29	30–34	35–39	40–44	45–49
Framework knitters						
Married under 25	$\frac{290}{714}$406	$\frac{198}{559}$331	$\frac{100}{401}$249	$\frac{46}{238}$193	$\frac{11}{108}$102	$\frac{1}{22}$45
Married Over 25		$\frac{44}{106}$415	$\frac{56}{160}$350	$\frac{35}{136}$257	$\frac{13}{91}$143	$\frac{1}{66}$15
		.80	.71	.75	.71	3.0
Others						
Married Under 25	$\frac{196}{415}$472	$\frac{136}{365}$373	$\frac{82}{240}$342	$\frac{26}{129}$202	$\frac{6}{65}$92	$\frac{0}{13}$0
Married Over 25		$\frac{21}{51}$412	$\frac{34}{97}$351	$\frac{25}{59}$424	$\frac{8}{48}$167	$\frac{0}{19}$0
		.91	.97	.48	.55	—

NOTE: In these calculations the numerator represents the total number of birth events, the denominator represents the total number of years that these women were "at risk" in each age group, and the product describes the age-specific fertility rate (per 1,000 years lived) of married women in each age group. The final row in each part represents the division of the product of the early marriers (under 25) by that of the late marriers (over 25).

tion study showed that the villagers marrying after 1825 were, to a greater extent than before, deliberately restricting their fertility as they grew older. The onset of this practice of fertility regulation was largely determined by the wife's age at marriage. In families in which the wife married before her twenty-fifth birthday, fertility rates were much lower, from the later twenties, than the fertility of later marrying women at comparable ages. In this instance, it is particularly fortunate that we are able to distinguish the behavior of the proto-industrialists from that of their fellow villagers. (See Table 3.)

The occupational influence in marital fertility strategies is very important. This evidence lends impressive support to the argument advanced earlier that reconciled the apparent contradiction between early marriage and high fertility in the first years of marriage, on the one hand, and, on the other, the deliberate practice of family limitation in the later years of marriage. We can now see that that demographic-economic explanation refers only to the behavior of the framework knitters. For the remainder of the villagers, the force of circumstances was quite different and so was the pattern of their fertility.

The information describing infant mortality presents a similar distinction between the experience of the proto-industrialists and the other members of the community. For this set of calculations we are able to analyze the issue two-dimensionally, both across time and within occupational groups (see Table 4).

The data in Table 4 show that practically the whole of the rise in infant mortality observed for the post-1825 cohort was experienced by the proto-industrialists. In contrast, the more traditional occupational groups suffered only a very slight increase. If we refer to the Ledermann tables and compare these infant mortality rates with his model mortality tables, we find that the initial life expectation (i.e., pre-1825) was about forty-four years for both groups. Yet the post-1825 life expectation at birth for the framework knitters fell to below thirty-six years while that of the rest of the community changed little. The observed mortality experience of the whole community therefore masks an important compositional variation.

Largely as a result of their increasing infant death rates the framework knitters' rate of replacement was substantially lower than that of the other villagers. The proto-industrialists' lower age at marriage was, as we have seen, more or less counterbalanced by their restricted fertility, which intensified as they grew older. For the agricultural laborers, village artisans, and shopkeepers, the economic opportunity unleashed by the first Industrial Revolution undermined the "prudential

TABLE 4. Infant Mortality Rates, by Parents' Occupation

Occupational Group	At Risk	Dying	Rate/1,000
Framework knitters			
1800–1824	1,013	161	159
1825–1849	606	135	223
Others			
1800–1824	535	87	163
1825–1849	226	38	168

NOTE: The experience of males and females has been added together.

check" that had previously enabled them to restrain their level of reproduction. Even after 1825 the rate of reproduction of these groups was by no means exceptional. Indeed, if we compare it with those attained by the villagers of Bottesford, Colyton, and Terling, we can see that it broadly conforms to an emerging pattern of population increase. In this light it was the framework knitters who were out of step with the prevailing demographic trends. For these proto-industrialists the tides of economic opportunity were ebbing—as was the age of nascent capitalism.

In his pioneering family reconstitution study of Colyton, Devon, E. A. Wrigley was primarily concerned with showing that significant variations in nuptiality, fertility, and mortality occurred in the period before the Industrial Revolution and the "demographic transition." It is unfortunate that Wrigley did not attempt to relate the substantial shifts in demographic behavior to the socioeconomic environment in which they occurred.

Before considering the relationship between economic opportunity and family formation, it might be helpful to review the salient aspects of Colyton's demographic history. Wrigley's choice of Colyton was propitious; the villagers displayed a remarkable variety of levels of nuptiality, fertility, and mortality. Age at marriage for men remained stable throughout the three hundred years of the study, but that for women changed dramatically. Of particular interest was the period when women married later (1647–1719) because it proved to be a time when women also consciously restricted fertility. In his masterful discussion of this phenomenon, Wrigley shows that fertility restriction was more stringent among those members of the cohort who married early, which is what we would expect to observe in a population aiming at a desired family size. Wrigley devoted most of his discussion to describing this period because the unexpected finding of deliberate family limitation together with rising age at marriage proved to be of such great interest.

Wrigley gave the years before 1647 and after 1719 relatively short shrift, although (or perhaps because) they were characterized by substantially higher levels of reproduction. The central finding of his study of nuptiality and fertility in Colyton was "not only that it was within the powers of preindustrial communities to halt population growth, but also that their powers of growth were very remarkable." In his study

Wrigley noted that there was "a well-marked inverse correlation between baptisms and burials until the end of the seventeenth century
which can still be detected at times in the eighteenth century."[7] Furthermore, "the pattern of change in adult death rates, as with the rates
for children, suggests a substantially lower expectation of life at birth in
the second half of the seventeenth century than in Elizabethan times
or Georgian England."[8] Thus, just as birth rates fluctuated, so death
rates varied also.

In interpreting the dramatic demographic discontinuity of the mid-
seventeenth century, Wrigley argued that the 1645–1646 epidemic of
the plague, which carried away perhaps one in five, was understood by
the villagers to be a warning—a danger signal against continued rapid
growth. The villagers' response was an adjustment of their demographic behavior to optimize their real incomes—later marriage and
fertility restriction, which were (involuntarily) abetted by higher mortality. In opposition to Wrigley's ascription of instinctive prudence, I
would argue that this demographic turnabout occurred in response to
the *deindustrialization* of Colyton.

In the later sixteenth century, Colyton conformed to Joan Thirsk's
model of a wood-pasture economy in which the rural textile industry
became well established. Small closes made ideal grazing ground on
intensively managed pastoral farms. Enclosure of subdivided arable
land in east Devon originated in the early middle ages. Most holdings
were fragmented; their scattered closes were small and elongated, fos-
silizing the preenclosure pattern of open-field strips. A survey of the
neighboring town of Axminster in 1574 reveals that the manor was
dominated by diminutive closes, and flooded meadows were so extensive that only 17 percent of the land was arable. In the seventeenth
century, east Devon surveys show that the average size of a close was
less than three acres. In east Devon this pattern was evident as late as
1796.[9]

Given these conditions it was logical for members of the agrarian
community to supplement their family incomes through cottage indus-

[7]Wrigley, "Family Limitation," p. 160, fn. 1, p. 193.
[8]Wrigley, "Mortality," p. 562.
[9]This paragraph is based on H. S. A. Fox, "The Chronology of Enclosure and Economic Development in Medieval Devon," *Economic History Review* 2d ser. 28, no. 2
(1975): 181–202.

try. Spinning, weaving, and finishing could be undertaken as subsidiary activities. Although such people could still be engaged in agrarian pursuits to garner a bare subsistence, domestic industry would provide them a margin above subsistence.[10] The productive capacity of an industry organized in this way would be determined largely by the duplication of productive units, not by technical efficiency. Available evidence suggests that this situation prevailed in Colyton during the later sixteenth century.[11]

In Elizabethan England the cloth trade boomed and the port of Exeter was a major export center. The trade of Exeter at this time consisted almost wholly of "Devon dozens" (i.e., kerseys), the traditional broadcloths produced in the region. In the early years of the seventeenth century the dominance of the broadcloths was challenged by the development of a new type of woolens—serges, woven from worsted and never milled. The emergence of the "new draperies" proved ideal for the export boom in the Mediterranean:[12] "At the turn of the [seventeenth] century the manufacture of serge in Devon had been negligible, in 1624 it was second only to the Devon dozens in Exeter's exports. The remarkable growth of Exeter's serge trade is illustrated beyond all doubt by a comparison of the export figures for the years before and after the Restoration. By 1647 the importance of serge is obvious and by 1666 it had become well established as Exeter's chief

[10] For this reason I believe that occupational information found in the parish register would be misleading. People who relied on a sideline to supplement their agricultural incomes would not be considered in determining the proportion of the population engaged in proto-industry. For people who lived on the edge of the agrarian system, the marginal addition to their family incomes provided by part-time spinning and weaving was what kept body and soul together. As the research of Pierre Goubert has shown us, such European peasants were not dissimilar to the Chinese peasantry before the Revolution, of whom R. H. Tawney wrote that "the position of the rural population is that of a man standing permanently up to the neck in water, so that even a ripple is sufficient to drown him" (*Land and Labour in China* [Boston: Beacon, 1966], p. 77). For a somewhat contrary view to the one presented here see E. A. Wrigley, "The Changing Occupational Structure of Colyton over Two Centuries," *Local Population Studies* 18 (Spring, 1977): 9–21.

[11] See, for example, the survey of Colyton conducted in the 1550s, which has several references to fulling mills and to "racks" used for stretching cloth (Devonshire Record Office 123/M/E/77).

[12] D. C. Coleman, "An Innovation and Its Diffusion: The 'New Draperies,'" *Economic History Review* 2d ser. 22, no. 3 (1969): 417–29.

export [indeed, by] the latter half of the [seventeenth] century all other types of cloth other than serge had become insignificant."[13]

Specialization of function was largely determined by the Exeter merchants who controlled the importation of raw Irish wool and the export of finished goods. Geography, too, played no small part in determining the structure and location of the various components of production. The logic of this geographical division of labor becomes clear when we realize that it was ideally suited to the capabilities of the existing transportation network. Spinning the raw wool at or near the port of entry insured that the pack trains traversing the north Devon moors carried a product ready for use. Moreover, by having the raw wool spun in isolated areas, the merchants were able to utilize the inexpensive "spare time" of farmers' and fishermen's wives and children. When the semiprocessed yarn was distributed to the weavers, the merchants could reckon on receiving a specified amount of woven fabric. In the weaving areas the workers were brought together into groups that bore a clear resemblance to "incipient factories." This concentration allowed the "agents" or "small masters" to maintain close supervision over production and thereby adjust quickly to changing fashions. Between the main weaving areas and the finishing centers of Exeter and Tiverton, communication was easy, making it relatively simple to transport the bulky woven, but as yet unfinished, cloth. The preeminence of Exeter in the finishing process and in mercantile activity can be explained largely by its position at the mouth of the river system running through central Devon.

As a result of this differentiation and stratification in the woolen industry, Colyton soon found itself on the outside looking in. Hoskins' study of the serge industry is accompanied by two maps clearly showing that the Blackdown Hills cut the Axe Valley off from the main areas of spinning and weaving. A more recent student of the cloth industry in seventeenth-century Devon, David Seward, has remarked on the critical role played by communication. He points out that Devon is noted for its rolling hills and steep valleys, which tend to interrupt communications, particularly from east to west. Because of this and

[13] W. B. Stephens, *Seventeenth Century Exeter* (Exeter: Exeter University Press, 1958), pp. 10, 103, 104.

the rainy climate, Devon roads consisted of steep inclines, bends and mud. Even by early seventeenth-century standards Devon roads were bad. The result of those physical barriers and poor communications seems to have been a separating of the various cloth-producing areas in the country and a hindering of their development as one economic unit.[14]

In his maps Hoskins notes all the places in Devon involved in the various processes in production of the "new draperies." Colyton is conspicuous by its absence. It may be suggested that the critical factor in Colyton's demise as an important woolen town was the shift to Irish wool that led to a radical restructuring of the geographical organization of local production. Thereafter, spinning and weaving continued in Colyton, to be sure, but they became vestigial.

The demographic effects of deindustrialization began when a type of employment that offered poor cottagers and husbandmen the chance to supplement their income was lost. Insofar as woolen production was a cornerstone of their household economies, the villagers lost a major source of income. In response to these changing economic conditions, they not only chose older brides but also restricted their family size. Furthermore, this demographic turnabout did not occur overnight, as Wrigley suggests. It was already in train in the first half of the seventeenth century—before the plague epidemic. During that period the woolen industry was already being reorganized, and the impact was felt in Colyton.

As the reorganization of the Devonshire cloth industry progressed, leaving Colyton high and dry, many young people deferred marriage or, more commonly, left the village to find better prospects elsewhere. After 1610 many potential marriages were frustrated, and young men and women were forced to leave their native hearth to find an economic environment in which they could marry and raise families within their modest expectations. This suggestion is supported by the long-term trend in the number of marriages celebrated annually in Colyton. From an annual average of about seven or eight per year in the 1560s, the curve moves upward until it peaks about the first decade of the seventeenth century when there was an average of about

[14] David Seward, "The Devonshire Cloth Industry in the Early Seventeenth Century," in *Industry and Society in the South-West*, ed. R. Burt, Exeter Papers in Economic History, vol. 3 (Exeter: Exeter University Press, 1970), pp. 31–50.

eighteen marriages per year in the village. From 1610 the trend moves downward, slowly at first, but then with an abrupt decline in the mid 1640s, after which it persists at a substantially lower level. The period that is of greatest interest from our present point of view is the early years of the seventeenth century when a long-term upward trend was reversed. (In many ways the absolute totals do not accurately reflect this demographic turnaround because they do not take into account the number of marriages that one would expect to occur if the long-term trend persisted. When a population is growing rapidly, the base of its age-pyramid expands, and the size of each succeeding cohort is substantially larger than its predecessor.) The implication of this phenomenon for our discussion of Colyton in the early seventeenth century is that not only was 1610, or thereabouts, the absolute end of the period of proto-industrial expansion and demographic growth, but it was also, and to a much greater extent, the relative end.

I have discussed the Colyton example at some length because this community's demographic cycle has, it seems to me, been misinterpreted. In explaining the dramatic drop in the villagers' net rate of reproduction I have stressed the influence of deindustrialization and have argued that the early seventeenth century in Colyton was a period of retrenchment in the face of diminishing economic opportunities. And it is the impact of these material conditions on marital strategies that must be considered if we are to discover the moving force behind the village's long-term reduction in its fertility and nuptiality during this period.

The implications of these proto-industrial developments were, I think, of great importance because they set in train a series of changes that ultimately cut the plebeian family adrift from the patriarchal control of social superiors and economic masters. Although it should be noted there was no significant change in the household structure of the cottage industrialists—almost everyone still lived in nuclear family units—there were some truly important changes within the home itself. In the proto-industrial centers the household became a focus for production in a way that it never was for agricultural laborers. Such work gave the worker control over the pace of production and, to a considerable extent, ownership of the means of production. Household units were multiplied in an effort to raise the volume of production. But the worker himself was allowed to dictate the pace of his work and the number of hours his wife and children were required to assist him. The three-day weekend with intermittent bouts of furious labor was a possibility during periods of high prices. At other times the family exploited itself and worked longer hours to maintain the accepted level of subsistence.[15] In many trades—textiles and small metalwares, in particular—the older children were kept at home so that they could contribute to the family's income. And at the critical stages in the family cycle when a surplus of infants threatened to sway the balance between mouths and hands, it was not unknown for apprentices (often orphaned paupers) to be brought into the household to restore an equilibrium. In a great many ways, the domestic economy of the proto-industrialists resembled that of the Russian peasantry described by Chayanov in the first part of the twentieth century.[16] Although they were engaged in the production of industrial products, their working life was determined by their own inner rhythms and not those of a modern economy. The notion that one worked to purchase consumer goods was only incompletely understood, and economic modernizers bewailed the fact that the leisure preference acted as a constant brake on the expansion of the forces of production.[17] And like the peasantry described by Chayanov, the family budget was adapted to the life cycle of its members because family work, and not simply the work of the chief breadwinner, was the rule.

In significant ways the proto-industrial laborer was a master in his own household who could take responsibility for organizing production and socializing children. Another way in which the freedom of the proto-industrial family differed from that of the agriculturalists was linked with the dispersed settlement pattern of rural industrial communities. For by and large rural domestic industries sprang up in communities that lacked strong patriarchal domination. In forest settle-

---

[15] This last phase of proto-industrialization provides some horrendous examples of self-exploitation—the handloom weavers, the framework knitters, and nailers were among the most steadfast "traditionalists" who would not suffer to lose their "independence" for a mess of pottage.

[16] A. V. Chayanov, *The Theory of the Peasant Economy* (Homewood, Ill.: Irwin, American Economic Association, 1966).

[17] D. C. Coleman, "Labour in the English Economy of the Seventeenth Century," *Economic History Review* 7, no. 3 (1956): 280–95. See also E. J. Hundert, "The Conception of Work and the Worker in Early Industrial England" (Ph.D. dissertation, University of Rochester, 1969), and Joyce Oldham Appleby, *Economic Thought and Ideology in Seventeenth Century England* (Princeton: Princeton University Press, 1978).

ments, freehold villages, and urban suburbs it was possible for these households to proliferate. The social and political implications of this lack of supervision were of real importance. It has been argued that both nonconformist religion and its Halévyan antithesis, radical politics, flourished in a seedbed of independent mechanics.[18] Such people were released from the patriarchal politics of the closed village. They had their own space in which to work and in which to think. They could interpret the world according to their own lights without the stern supervision of an old priest or new presbyter. The radical religion of the lower classes stressed free will and individual responsibility. Not surprisingly John Bunyan was a "mechanic preacher," and John Wesley found some of his most enthusiastic converts among the Cornish tin miners and the northeastern colliers. The opportunity for intellectual independence afforded by this proto-industrial mode of production was crucial to the emergence of a world view that was not interpreted through the patriarchal organization of knowledge.

The growth of this plebeian army of proto-industrialists was largely underwritten by their own "prolific power." It would seem that rural industry played a crucial role in undermining the prudential and restrictive reproductive regime of the preindustrial world. By permitting, one might even say promoting, a multiplication of productive units—each based on a separate household—the old nexus of patriarchal control over marriage was broken. Men and women could contemplate marriage in the knowledge that their "independence" was not granted by a supervening authority. Marriage could be undertaken with reference to a system in which they sold the products of their labor. There were no restrictions about entry into such a marketplace. So-called beggar marriages were frequent. What is more, the average age at marriage dropped dramatically, bringing with it an increase in the period of time women were liable to bear children within marriage. As the age at marriage fell so, too, did the period of time between generations. There is also some slight evidence to suggest that marital fertility rose as well—perhaps because of the difficulty working mothers (particularly young ones) had in breast-feeding their small children, and therefore in maintaining a long anovulatory period. It is quite clear that the combined effect of earlier and more frequent mar-

[18] Alan Everitt, *The Pattern of Rural Dissent*, Department of English, Local History, Occasional Papers, 2d ser., no. 4 (Leicester: Leicester University Press, 1972).

riage together with a marginally higher level of marital fertility were not counterbalanced by a drastic rise in mortality. The result was that the replacement rate of proto-industrialists far outstripped the previous levels known in the earlier epoch. An additional factor contributing to the higher population growth rates among the rural workers was illegitimacy. Paradoxically, the earlier women married the more likely they were to be pregnant at marriage. It does not appear that frustration with the postponement of sexual relations until marriage, some ten years after puberty, was, by itself, a cause of rampant promiscuity. The new strategy unveiled in the proto-industrial areas allowed for sexual intercourse before marriage, which, unfortunately, resulted in unwed mothers at a time when economic conditions made it difficult to set up another productive unit. In a very real sense, the proto-industrialists predicated their sexual behavior on the continuation of economic growth. When the economy was sluggish such plans were upset, although the sexual anticipation of marriage did leave many young women in the lurch. The planned marriage not infrequently took place when conditions improved.

The quickening pace of economic growth began in the middle of the eighteenth century when all the indicators rose concurrently: population, industrial production, aggregate demand, and so on. But if we shift our gaze from the reams of statistics to the lives of those individuals who experienced this process, it is less clear that we can pinpoint any definite change. Rather what we see is a superimposition of new forms of life and work. But it will not do to see this compositional shift occurring at the expense of proto-industrial organization of family labor. For, as I have already mentioned, the family mode of production carried on. It carried on not only at home but also in the workshops and factories that sprang up.[19] The first factory proletariat was a motley

[19] N. J. Smelser, *Social Change in the Industrial Revolution* (Chicago: University of Chicago Press, 1959); Michael Anderson, "Sociological History and the Working-class Family: Smelser Revisited," *Social History* 3 (1976): 317–34; and M. M. Edwards and P. Lloyd-Jones, "N. J. Smelser and the Cotton Factory Family: A Reassessment," in *Textile History and Economic History*, ed. N. B. Harte and N. C. Ponting (Manchester: Manchester University Press, 1973), pp. 304–19. It would appear that the key to the debate that Smelser initiated more than two decades ago is to be found in Anderson's discussion of it. He states that "Smelser's typical picture is of a spinner recruiting his own children as piecers, and this may well have been the ideal, and *was probably, indeed, a usual phase in the life-cycle of almost all spinners until long after 1851* [italics added]. It can never, however, have been the dominant pattern at any one time for, given the age

assortment of rootless artisans, women, and parish pauper children. No one else would work hour after hour, day after day, week after week, year after year. The rhythms of an earlier world of work were not so easily superseded. In this era of growing population, orphans and pauper children were in abundant supply, and the factories provided an outlet to relieve parishes swollen with high welfare rolls. The crying need during the first generation of full-scale industrialization was for workers who were able to adapt themselves to the regular pace of the power-driven machines. When these factory children married, they seem to have tried to recreate the family mode of production beside the power-driven machines. Master spinners preferred to employ their own children, but for only a brief time in the course of their working lives did they have the right number to fill the positions assisting them. Thus, while the master spinner might employ all his children for as long as possible, at any one point in time a "snapshot" would show that not only were most children not employed by their parents, but that most adults were not employing their own children. Seen from the longitudinal perspective of the factory family's life cycle, however, it is possible to understand that such "snapshots" might be profoundly misrepresentative. The crucial point is that the factory family was able to recreate the family work unit for periods of time and that this family mode of production was the ideal type against which other variants were measured. Only with the introduction of self-acting machinery in the 1830s—some sixty-five years after the first spinning factory opened—was the paternal role as the organizer of the work team supervened. In the course of these three generations, a major industrial conurbation had sprung up in southeast Lancashire, centering on Manchester, and many, many thousands of fathers, mothers, and children were to be found working side by side for those stages in the life cycle when it proved feasible. While the residential unit was still overwhelmingly nuclear in its composition, there is some evidence to suggest that the prevalence of early marriage, the lack of housing, and the difficulty of surviving on one wage packet were associated with an increase in coresidence for a short period after marriage when the young couple was most burdened with dependents. The

distribution of the spinning population, rather few spinners would *ever* have had enough children of a suitable age to piece for them" (p. 325). Seen in this way the objections of Edwards and Lloyd-Jones are almost beside the point.

need to balance hands and mouths dictated the size and composition of the household. Such needs fluctuated over the family cycle and so, too, did women's involvement in industrial labor.[20] The urban industrial environment created new opportunities for wagework, and the working-class family experimented with a wide variety of strategies over the course of its life together.

Although migration was a significant factor in the growth of the factory proletariat, the demographic profile of the working class created a massive reservoir of potential labor power. In essence, it appears that the women marrying factory workers were young, like the proto-industrialists' brides, and that they had high levels of fertility. The infant and child mortality rates in the new urban agglomerations were dreadful, but nevertheless, the high birth rates in the city centers, the suburbs, the small towns, and the proto-industrial villages were able to overcome even those tragic statistics so that the industrial working class reproduced itself at a rapid pace.

Demographic factors were not only a response to economic changes, they also influenced them. The vast massing of labor that was generated by the proletarian demography model created the conditions that underpinned the very dramatic shift in the social distribution of wealth and particularly income. By glutting the labor market, the proletarians' very own reproductive strategies created the economic conditions in which proto-industry could flourish and, by flourishing, perpetuate the process during the nascent capitalist period. Finally, the vitality of proto-industrial forms of production was absolutely critical to the ultimate success of capitalist relations of production. Proto-industry was a more profitable form of production than manufacturing artisans' works in that the laborers bore many of the capital risks, such as they were, inasmuch as labor and not fixed capital was the primary ingredient in most productive processes. Insofar as proto-industrialists were isolated and had few institutional or even geographical bases for communal resistance to the wage-fixing practices of merchant capital-

---

[20] Generally speaking, women worked before marriage and then for a short time thereafter, but gradually withdrew from the labor force as domestic responsibilities and the wage-earning of older children transformed the burden of the family economy. Older women with adult or teen-age children went back to work in relatively small numbers. It would appear that older women more often contributed by taking in boarders and lodgers or by doing piecework. See Louise A. Tilly and John W. Scott, *Women, Work and Family* (New York: Holt, Rinehart and Winston, 1978).

ists, the success of proto-industry was the obverse aspect of the production by artisans or guilds.

It was the proliferation of consumer goods that distinguished the proto-industrial manufacturing sector and provided the thrust behind the "take off"; as an isolated, time-specific event, it is necessary to regard the process of proto-industrialization as a long and drawn-out development. The household mode of production and the small subcontracting workshop were but two aspects of this development. They were quite different from the factory enterprises in which workers sold their labor time and not the products of their labor. The distinction is a crucial one because on it hinges the difference between the proto-industrial mode of production and its successor, which was based on high fixed-capital expenditures and the purchase of labor power to service the machinery. In the mature form of capitalist production men and women became adjuncts to the regular, inanimately powered machines. They sold their labor and their time for a wage. For many who were caught up in this process, it was indeed a species of slavery. However, in the second quarter of the nineteenth century most production was not based on this model. Most workers followed older rhythms and worked in quite different conditions.

It is very clear that the final stages of the nascent capitalist era, after 1770, also witnessed the growth of forces that would break apart the proto-industrial mode of production. But the crucial fact, it appears to me, is that this proto-industrial mode carried on in many sectors of the manufacturing economy. It not only carried on, it flourished. These years, 1770–1850, witnessed the final Indian summer for the proto-industrial mode of production. Proletarian family formation was largely predicated on the availability of work for children and the existence of a family wage economy. As ties with the land were attenuated and then irreparably severed among the inhabitants of mushrooming industrial villages, towns, and cities, it became imperative to purchase goods that had previously been available from common lands, tenement gardens, and small holdings. The final stage of proto-industrialization was marked by the intensification of the distinction between production for exchange and production for use. The family economy was almost completely proletarianized as the family had to sell the products of its labor in order to purchase necessities. This final stage of proto-industrialization was marked by the intensification of

child labor in mines, nailing communities, framework knitting villages
and the weaving hamlets, as well as the infamous London slop trades.
Many of the grievous social ills of the early Industrial Revolution resulted from the involution of the proto-industrial family economy.[21]

[21] Earlier in this essay and in *Family Formation* I characterized the social and economic deterioration of living conditions among the mid-nineteenth-century framework
knitters as a form of "industrial involution" (pp. 33–34). The concept is, of course, bor-
rowed from Clifford Geertz, *Agricultural Involution: The Process of Ecological Change
in Indonesia* (New York: Basic Books, 1978).

Infirmities of the Body and Vices of the Soul: Migrants, Family, and Urban Life in Turn-of-the-Century France

"Men are made not to be crowded into anthills but to be dispersed over the earth," intoned Rousseau in 1762. "The more they come together the more they are corrupted. The infirmities of the body as well as the vices of the soul are the unfailing effect of this overcrowding. . . . Cities are the abyss of the human species. At the end of a few generations, the races perish or degenerate. They must be renewed and it is always the country which provides for this renewal."[1] When Rousseau contrasted the healthy, life-giving countryside with the physically and morally destructive city, he set the theme for the French a century later. By the end of the nineteenth century, concern with unhealthy urban life spread as the mass exit from countryside to city—now baptized "the rural exodus"—became a national concern. For many, cities represented vice and the countryside, virtue.

Physical conditions of urban life justified widespread concern. The working-class family correctly appeared to be the primary victim, for the destructive elements of city life were particularly ruinous to the family. Unhealthy water and crowded housing in urban areas, for example, promoted high rates of infant mortality and tuberculosis. Alcoholism and high rates of illegitimacy and divorce likewise threatened the stability and health of urban families. Most susceptible to the dangers of the city was the dazzled and helpless newcomer—the migrant newly arrived, "uprooted from the earth, chased from the flatlands by

Many thanks to Nora Faires, Kathleen Underwood, and Gary Stark for their helpful comments on an earlier version of this essay. I am grateful to Louise Tilly for loaning me the data for Amiens and Roubaix and to Cathy Whitaker for performing its analysis after completing the arduous task of adapting that data to my needs.

[1] Jean-Jacques Rousseau, *Emile or On Education*, trans. Allan Bloom (New York: Basic Books, 1978), p. 59.

the agricultural crisis, conscripted by the barracks, store and factory, [and] hypnotized by the city lights like the sea birds who, after sunset, fly bewildered under the beam of the lighthouse."[2] Concerned observers of city life between 1850 and 1914 judged the city to be a "devourer of men" and the newcomer to the city to be something of a lost soul.

Yet historians of the family share this view less and less as the "ghosts of social breakdown are being exorcised from historical scholarship" on the urban family.[3] In fact, historians are reaching the opposite conclusion—that families were less the victims of urban growth and more its agent. Studies of the factory city in Europe and North America have revealed chains of migrants from a particular rural area bound together by ties of kinship and friendship. Migration to industrial Lancashire, argued Michael Anderson a decade ago, actually led to increased dependence on kin.[4] Likewise, Tamara Hareven concluded that "individuals and families migrating into cities or already living in them relied on relatives or former townsmen as sources of support or sociability."[5] Evidence from industrial towns in particular supports the view that "migration to the city was often undertaken within family and kinship networks, or by whole families."[6] The support of migration by the family is amounting to a new orthodoxy.

Consequently, we are now in possession of two views of the migrants' family life and the effect of the city upon it. On the one hand, concerned observers in pre–World War I Europe ascertained that the city destroyed people's ability to marry, raise healthy children, remain healthy themselves, or to maintain a marriage. On the other hand, today's historians who study the family see a group that tenaciously stayed together as people moved from rural to urban areas. The few working-class memoirs that do exist tend to support the second view, that families stayed together and that kin depended on one another

[2] Emile Vandervelde, *L'exode rural et le retour aux champs* (Paris: Alcan, 1903), pp. 18–19. This quote and others from French works are translated by the author.

[3] Tamara Hareven, "Family Time and Industrial Time: Family and Work in a Planned Corporation Town," *Journal of Urban History* 1, no. 3 (May, 1975): 360.

[4] Michael Anderson, *Family Structure in Nineteenth Century Lancashire* (Cambridge: Cambridge University Press, 1971), pp. 177–78.

[5] Tamara Hareven, "The Historical Study of the Family in Urban Society," *Journal of Urban History* 1, no. 3 (May, 1975): 263.

[6] Gordon Darroch, "Migrants in the Nineteenth Century: Fugitives or Families in Motion?" *Journal of Family History* 6, no. 3 (Fall, 1981): 257.

in the face of the difficulties presented by urban life. The existence of two views of the family in the growing city is significant because those views represent separate realities in the human experience of urbanization.

This essay attempts to reconcile the separate realities of the nineteenth-century reformer and today's historian. It reports an investigation of reformers' concerns with family life in three growing French cities and turns to the sources of today's historian for information on family life. Finally, it focuses on the contradictions and points of agreement between the two views. The study investigates three cities to show a range of effects, because all cities were probably not alike in their impact on the newcomer's family. Some may have allowed and encouraged kin to stay together. Although most historians' information on urban family life comes from factory towns, factories and textile mills were not the most important employers in pre–World War I Europe. Rather, most urban dwellers worked in small workshops, stores, or in the homes of other people. As a consequence, the factory city gives an incomplete view of urban life.

This investigation of reformers' views and migrants' family lives will cover three distinct French cities: picturesque Amiens in the north, home of a declining textile trade; the ancient city of Nîmes in the south, a commercial center; and Roubaix, a factory city near the Belgian border. It will become apparent that reformers' concerns were not the same for every city because each city had different problems and that the family was not destroyed. But particular cities influenced families in different ways because some encouraged families to move together, live together, and work together; the textile mill town, for example, promoted family solidarity for working-class newcomers in ways that commercial and administrative cities could not.

The Cities and Reformers' Concerns

Amiens, capital of the ancient region of Picardy, is located at a bend in the Somme River about eighty miles north of Paris. Like many of France's cities, its origins lie in its use as a passageway. In the case of Amiens, the river divides into small streams, creating an easy crossing point that was used by both Celts and Romans. By the seventeenth century the city was fed by people from the surrounding countryside and from the plains of northern France that were tied with Amiens by the production of cloth that characterized the region from Normandy north to the Ruhr. The city's imposing Gothic cathedral, its old city, and its honorable past set it apart from the new factory towns of the nineteenth century: in Amiens one still could sense "the charm of moss-covered cottages or the calm majesty of cathedrals."[7]

Indeed, Amiens was a city geared to life before the Industrial Revolution. Although it was a capital of the textile industry, it was more a place of exchange than of production, because most cloth actually was produced in villages. The densely populated countryside divided its labors between the field and cottage; when not working the land, rural families produced hand-loomed cloth. Spinning and weaving were the vocations of the countryside and the processing of fabric—the fulling, dyeing, and finishing—occurred in the city.[8]

Amiens' role as a capital for cottage industry would be important in the era of mechanized industry and rural exodus. First, home production was cheap for the entrepreneur who did not have the expense of a factory or even the spinning wheel or loom. The resistance of Amiens' bourgeoisie to these investments meant that the city could not compete in the race to produce goods of the quality and quantity possible with mechanized looms.[9] And the goods of Amiens were produced *en famille*: "Each family works on its piece until it is completed, the wife replacing the husband, the adolescent daughter taking the place of the mother as needed. This is a family apprenticeship. From the winding of thread, which falls to the children, to the assembly [of cloth,] which is the work of the father or of boys trained under him, everything is prepared and completed in the home."[10] Some claimed that a concern for the workers' family was the reason Amiens was slow to modernize, reasoning that "towns with their taxes and cabarets are at once a costly residence and a bad school for workers."[11]

---

[7] Pierre Deyon, *Amiens, capitale provinciale: Étude sur la société urbaine au XVIIe siècle* (Paris: Mouton, 1967), pp. 8–10, 349–50; Louis Reybaud, *La laine* (Paris: Lévy, 1867), p. 221; Albert Demangeon, *La Picardie*, 4th ed. (Paris: Guenegaud, 1973), pp. 388–89.

[8] Demangeon, *La Picardie*, pp. 400–10; Louis Reybaud, *Le coton: Son régime, ses problems. Son influence en Europe* (Paris: Lévy, 1863), p. 227.

[9] Reybaud, *Le coton*, pp. 220–23.

[10] Reybaud, *La laine*, p. 223.

[11] Reybaud, *Le coton*, p. 162.

Nineteenth-century Amiens saw no sharp division between urban and rural life. Nearby rural areas were not purely agricultural by any means. They were engaged in the manufacturing of cloth, and the part of Picardy not engaged in textile production often turned out bricks or metalwork. Moreover, agriculture was an important part of the city's economy. The Somme River and its canals formed small islands in the city, whose rich soil supported prosperous market gardens called *hortillons*. Shallow boats carried the gardener and produce to market. Radishes, lettuce, carrots, onions, and leeks planted in February were harvested from May to August. In August cabbage and more lettuce were planted. Cherry, plum, apple, and pear trees complemented the city's vegetables.[12] Agricultural work, then, was part of urban life, and industrial production was a part of village life.

As a consequence, the rural people of Picardy had long been a part of the economy of Amiens when the rural exodus began. It was not strangers who populated the city as it grew; rather, one citizen reported, "Neighboring regions pour unceasingly into Amiens workers' families and white-collar families, eager to exchange the hard labor of the countryside or the modest resources of the small town for the seductions of the grand hospitable city."[13] Indeed, nearly four out of five migrants in Amiens in 1906 were from the region, and almost half the people in town were migrants—that is, they had been born outside the city.[14] As cottage industry failed because it could not compete with the even quality and low price of mechanically produced textiles, the countryside of Picardy emptied and its small towns withered. There was a direct link between decreasing village populations and the stilling of rural looms. For example, at the beginning of the century, the village of Villers-Bocage (population 1,193) seven miles north of Amiens supported 150 textile workers (*écorchers*). A century later the workers were gone and the population had shrunk to 824.[15]

Urban industry attracted some migrants to Amiens. The production of velours and corduroy did survive into the twentieth century and

[12] Robert Fossier, *Histoire de la Picardie* (Toulouse: Privat, 1974), pp. 364–65.

[13] Alberic de Calonne d'Avesne, *Histoire de la ville d'Amiens*, vol. 3 (1906; reprint ed., Marseille: Lafitte Reprints, 1976), p. 435.

[14] This figure is taken from a 10 percent sample of households from the 1906 census lists of Amiens, which includes birthplace.

[15] Demangeon, *La Picardie*, pp. 407–409.

some factories were built on the outskirts of town. Yet the textile industry stagnated and other areas of the city economy expanded.[16] Two new industries, manufacturing of shoes and of men's ready-to-wear clothing, developed at the end of the nineteenth century. Some were employed in such industries as metallurgy. The railroad employed many more, because Amiens became a point of intersection for rail lines from Paris to Belgium and to ports and resorts on the English Channel. Given this impetus, commerce increased and provided jobs for workers from the unskilled hauler to white-collar clerk to wholesale merchant. And as the importance of public services and government employment increased after 1850, Amiens' function as prefecture of the Department of the Somme meant more clerical and professional jobs in its courthouse, tax offices, road offices, and schools. Many government employees were not natives of the region, but were sent to Amiens by the national bureaucracy. Thus colonies formed of functionaries without great local attachment.[17]

The city grew, bursting the belt of its old walls and spreading up away from the Somme River. By the turn of the century, Amiens stretched four miles along the river, and its outlying areas grew as the rural population of Picardy decreased. In place of the fifty-two thousand people there in 1851, over ninety thousand lived in Amiens in 1906.

Despite its expansion, the prospects for the family in Amiens were dismal, because the city was notorious for poxes upon family life such as unhealthy housing, a high proportion of illegitimate births, and alcoholism. The housing in the textile workers' neighborhoods down on the river was particularly unhealthy because the dampness required by weavers and the river waters on which dyers and fabric finishers depended made the air heavy in their low houses. The dwellings emitted a "nauseating odor," according to an 1860s' report.[18] This housing became increasingly crowded because the working population of Amiens almost doubled during the reign of Napoleon III, but the number of houses in Amiens hardly increased. For middle-class observers,

---

[16] Calonne d'Avesne, *Amiens*, p. 433; Demangeon, *La Picardie*, p. 416; Fossier, *Picardie*, pp. 378–79.

[17] Fossier, *Picardie*, p. 380.

[18] Jules Simon, *L'ouvrière* (Paris: Hachette, 1861), quoted in Reybaud, *La laine*, p. 237.

crowded housing represented a shocking promiscuity: "In this space of a few square feet an entire family is parked; ages and sexes are mixed; the beds are used in common without a partition or even a curtain separating them. For childhood and adolescence, this is a sad apprenticeship in decency."[19] Housing remained unsanitary and crowded into the twentieth century in Amiens' old town, an area in which unhealthy slums were piled around damp and narrow courts. Fortunately, new housing expanded with the city as two- and four-room houses, many with a garden in back, sprouted on the hills in new suburbs.[20]

The most direct challenge Amiens delivered to the family was that marriages would not occur at all and that illegitimate children would never be legally recognized by their fathers (who would, therefore, never have legal financial responsibility for them). Although high rates of illegitimacy are part of a northern French pattern, Amiens was singled out for high proportions of bastard children as early as the 1830s when one child in seven was illegitimate. As an attempt to stem the tide of illegitimacy, the St. Charles hospital began to supervise closely the admission of foundlings after 1850. This merely increased the number of women supporting children alone on their meager salaries. Reformers continued to bemoan the high proportion of bastard children, and the department's illegitimate births continued to increase through the last decades of the century.[21]

Amiens' greatest vice was drunkeness. It was, with one exception, the town most noted for drunkenness in France in the 1860s. In a country quite unconcerned with alcoholism, where temperance movements experienced none of the successes they enjoyed in Anglo-Saxon nations, the drinking habits of Amiens' population attracted early attention. The first temperance society in the nation was founded in the 1830s in Amiens, but its members were few and it quietly died in a few years. "Barkeeps," concluded Reybaud in 1867, "remain the masters of the terrain." An estimated eighty thousand glasses of brandy were imbided daily—about a glass and a half for every man, woman, and child

[19] Calonne d'Avesne, *Amiens*, p. 317; Reybaud, *Le coton*, p. 230.

[20] Calonne d'Avesne, *Amiens*, pp. 317–18, 435; Fossier, *Picardie*, p. 376; Reybaud, *La laine*, pp. 237–43.

[21] R. Burr Litchfield and David Gordon, "Closing the 'Tour': A Close Look at the Marriage Market, Unwed Mothers, and Abandoned Children in Mid-nineteenth Century Amiens," *Journal of Social History* 13, no. 3 (Spring, 1980): 458–73.

in the city.[22] And because the citizens did not drink such fermented beverages as beer or wine (that pillar of the national economy) but preferred distilled alcohol, theirs was perceived to be a particularly brutish drunkenness.[23] It kept the man at the cabaret and the woman at home to deal with work orders and children's need for food and care. If the family nourishment had a claim on the family budget, so did the cabaret, but, observed Audiganne: "Since it is the cabaret client who presides over the division [of family resources], he too often consecrates a weak sum to domestic needs, sometimes keeping more than half for himself. The wife manages as best she can; in other words, the hearth is without fire and the children beg in the streets covered with rags."[24]

British investigators who studied the standard of living of French working people in 1905 found that wages were low, yet the cost of food in Amiens was as high as in Paris. Income of workers in Amiens was never adequate to provide food and shelter for a couple with children.[25] These economic conditions must have contributed to the persistence of slums in some parts of town. In addition, the difficulty of supporting a family probably discouraged marriage and encouraged illegitimacy. And although poverty does not explain the national trend of hard drinking at the end of the nineteenth century, it certainly may have contributed to Amiens' long-lived penchant for brandy.

The reputation of the city of Nîmes, its climate, and its physical environment, all offer a contrast to Amiens. Nîmes is located on the broad plain that separates the Mediterranean Sea from the central

[22] Susanna Barrows, "After the Commune: Alcoholism, Temperance, and Literature in the Early Third Republic," in *Consciousness and Class Experience in Nineteenth-Century Europe*, ed. John Merriman (New York: Holmes and Meier, 1979); Reybaud, *La laine*, p. 236.

[23] Michael Marrus, "Social Drinking in the Belle Epoque," *Journal of Social History* 7, no. 2 (Winter, 1974): 115–41.

[24] Armand Audiganne, *Les populations ouvrières et les industries de la France*, vol. 2, 2d ed. (1860; reprint ed., New York: Burt Franklin, 1970), p. 40.

[25] Great Britain, Board of Trade, *Cost of Living in French Towns. Report of an Inquiry of the Board of Trade into Working Class Rents, Housing and Retail Prices, Together with the Rates of Wages in Certain Occupations in the Principal Industrial Towns of France*. Presented to both Houses of Parliament by Command of His Majesty, Cd 4512, 1909, pp. 37, 44; Louise Tilly and Steven Dubnoff, "Families and Wage Earning in Amiens and Roubaix, 1906: Measures of Income Adequacy and Household Response in Two French Cities," Paper delivered at the Annual Meeting of the Social Science History Association, 1978, Columbus, Ohio, pp. 7–8.

highlands of France west of the Rhone River. It was founded by the Celts because its spring gave relief to the region's hot, dry landscape. The Romans chose to make Nemausis (as they called it) an important city and built temples as well as an arena that is used to this day. In the nineteenth century, the city's walls were razed and boulevards were created that acted as a belt surrounding the old city. Outlying areas, settled before the Revolution, filled in and expanded as the city grew from fifty to eighty thousand in the second half of the nineteenth century.[26]

Nîmes' population came from its mountainous hinterland. The Cévennes mountain range that rises from the plain and the more remote central highlands of France had provided a seemingly inexhaustible supply of people since the middle ages. Mountain people resuscitated the plague-depleted cities of the plain in the fourteenth century; they appeared as beggars and workers in search of food and warmth in the sixteenth. The deaths of many are recorded in regional hospitals, but others thrived, or at least survived, and stayed on to forge a single region of plain and mountain called Languedoc.[27]

In the eighteenth century, Nîmes became an industrial city, producing cloth and hose from raw silk manufactured on the plain and in the Cévennes mountains. Weavers and their families populated the city; when Thomas Jefferson sat in admiration before the Roman temple called the Maison Carrée in 1787, he was surrounded by young girls who spun and knit in the sunlight. This industry, however, did not survive the nineteenth century for, in the words of a contemporary, "the South was defeated in this battle" for industrial progress.[28] After 1860 even the production of fashionable shawls foundered. Competition from the north and a disease decimating silkworms and silk production played their role in the deindustrialization of Nîmes.[29]

A decision of the bourgeoisie was also crucial to the city's loss of industry. Many abandoned industry to become land-holding vintners because of the profits to be gained in the grape harvest and wine mar-

---

[26] Leslie Page Moch, *Paths to the City: Regional Migration in Nineteenth-Century France* (forthcoming), chap. 3.

[27] Fernand Braudel, *La Méditerrannée et le monde Méditerranéen à l'époque de Philippe II* (Paris: Armand Colin, 1949), pp. 272–74; Emmanuel LeRoy Ladurie, *Les paysans de Languedoc* (Paris: S.E.V.P.E.N., 1966), pp. 98–102.

[28] Reybaud, *Le coton*, p. 157.

[29] Moch, *Paths to the City*, chap. 3.

ket: "The vinyard killed true industry. . . . The transformation of lower Languedoc into a wine factory is in a great part responsible for the deindustrialization of the region."[30]

Nîmes developed as a trade and commercial center rather than an industrial producer by the twentieth century. Like the people of Amiens, the citizens of Nîmes augmented this trading function with two new industries of clothing and shoe manufacture. And like Amiens, Nîmes served as a railroad entrepôt and the prefecture of the department. Consequently, both Nîmes and Amiens offered employment in commerce, transportation, and services.

If its vocation was similar to that of Amiens, its society was not, for Nîmes was a center for Protestantism. Although France was an overwhelmingly Catholic nation, about a third of Nîmes' people in 1850 were Protestants, with ties to the Cévennes mountains that had hidden Huguenot refugees from Louis XIV's armies in the seventeenth century. During the nineteenth century, however, the Protestant population of the city was diluted by newcomers from the more remote hinterland of Nîmes, the staunchly Catholic central highlands.[31] The city was only a quarter Protestant by the turn of the century. Nevertheless, Protestants left a distinctive stamp on Nîmes and were more influential than their numbers suggest. They were disproportionally represented in the bourgeoisie and among clerical workers.[32] Moreover, a liberal tradition forged their political views while royalist politics influenced Catholics even after monarchists ceased to be an important force in French politics.[33] Differences in style of living added a cultural element to economic and political differences; in 1900 Nîmes was a city of two cultures.

The existence of competing faiths provided two concerned ministries to the family. The effect of old and dilapidated housing on health

---

[30] Raymond Dugrand is quoted in Philippe Wolff, *Histoire du Languedoc* (Toulouse: Privat, 1967), p. 501.

[31] Moch, *Paths to the City*, chap. 3; Jean-Daniel Roque, "Nouveaux aperçus sur l'Eglise protestante de Nîmes dans la séconde moitié du XIXe siècle," *Bulletin de la Société de l'Histoire du Protestantisme* 120 (1974): 54, 55, 57.

[32] Moch, *Paths to the City*, chap. 3; Roque, "L'Eglise protestante de Nîmes," pp. 68–70.

[33] Leo Loubère, *Radicalism in Mediterranean France: Its Rise and Decline, 1848–1914* (Albany: State University of New York Press, 1974), pp. 57, 136–38, 199, and Moch, *Paths to the City*, chap. 3.

and morals concerned both Protestants and Catholics. The old city's worst houses were destroyed, yet suburbs offered little relief. "Certainly," wrote a concerned pastor, "it was correct to eliminate the litter of disgusting alleyways which occupied the present site of the central market. . . . But the workers and the poor who lived there, about whom there was hardly any concern, were compressed into the outlying areas and had to crowd into veritable slums."[34] An artisan raised in a dilapidated building in the old city that was several hundred years old recalled that the "low and entangled workers' houses in the outlying areas with their multiple stairways, their long dirty corridors, their interior courts, were no more disagreeable than ours."[35] Indeed, the major difference between rich and poor was not food or nutrition in Nîmes, but lodging; while bourgeois apartments were vast, high ceilinged, and well lit, those of artisans, shopkeepers, and workers were small and often untouched by sunlight. Most people lived in two rooms, one which served as shop, kitchen, dining room, and living room, the other as bedroom. An alcove—invariably without a window—might be partitioned off for a child. In city and suburb, a common well and a common toilet served the entire building.[36] Consequently, the death rate in Nîmes varied by neighborhood—more specifically by the size of lodgings, the width of streets, number of windows, and quantity and quality of water for inhabitants.[37]

Some plagues of family life did not jeopardize the people of Nîmes. Traditionally, they had few illegitimate children. Indeed, the illegitimacy rate for Nîmes was less than half that of Amiens.[38] Moreover, the people in Nîmes did not have reputations as great drinkers because they drank very little distilled liquor. They may have consumed vast amounts of the local wine, but wine did not produce alcoholism in the view of the time; it merely promoted a lighthearted and thoroughly Gallic inebriation. Bars were the robber of the family's time and money and represented a greater problem than alcohol itself.[39]

[34] Louis Trial, "Un ennemi de la famille: Le logement insalubre," *Revue du Midi* (1900): 950.

[35] Paul Marcelin, *Souvenirs d'un passé artisanal* (Nîmes: Chastanier, 1967), p. 17.

[36] Ibid., pp. 10, 22, 23; Trial, "Un ennemi de la famille," p. 948.

[37] Elie Mazel, "Statistique démographique de la ville de Nîmes comparée (1876–1888)," *Mémoires de l'Académie de Nîmes*, 7th ser. 10 (1887): 251–52.

[38] Ibid., p. 225.

[39] Marrus, "Social Drinking," p. 120.

Nîmes was not without vice, however, and migrants, women in particular, were accused of playing an overactive role in the city's immorality. Writing about the prostitutes of Nîmes, a local doctor characterized them as "illiterate girls, peasants and *montagnardes*, servants for the most part [and] vicious, gluttonous and lazy on top of everything else."[40] The civil servant who managed the municipal employment agency that primarily served rural women looking for work as domestic servants vindictively ranted against his clientele: "Inured to all the dangers inherent in their kind and in their profession, for selfish motives and in this somewhat idle existence they quickly take up lazy habits. Then they become the familiars of the employment agencies, alternating their professional work with occupations of a different order."[41]

Much concern about the urban family in Nîmes was focused on the city's demographic configuration, which was similar to the country in general and concerned the entire nation. France's low birthrate caused considerable dismay, and after defeat at the hands of the Germans in 1870, the consternation increased because the birthrate in Germany was considerably higher than that in France. This meant that Germany's population was younger and more vigorous than that of France and that it was producing soldiers at a greater rate. In a nation of few children, Nîmes cut a particularly sad figure, for it produced even fewer children per capita than other urban centers such as Paris, Marseille, or Amiens. The French family would expire for want of children. If it were ever formed, that is, for in Nîmes, "They hardly marry," complained a doctor in the 1880s.[42] Even the people of Paris and Amiens were more likely to form families. Indeed, Nîmes appeared to contemporaries as an extreme case in face of the nation's concern with the future of the French race, specifically because marriages were rare and families small.

Roubaix, the final city examined in this essay, stands in contrast to Nîmes and Amiens on almost every dimension. A center of factory industry and a city that sprang from a small town, Roubaix lacked the traditions of urban settlement and regional population supply of either

[40] Mazel, "Statistique démographique," p. 265.

[41] Municipal Archives of Nîmes, Annual Report of Municipal Employment Agency, 1904, Series F-7, 55, 2.

[42] Mazel, "Statistique démographique," pp. 221–24.

Amiens or Nîmes. No Roman roads traversed this corner of Gaul, and the Germanic origins of the city's name suggest it was not founded until the seventh or eighth century. More important, in 1815 Roubaix was a town of merely eight thousand, indistinguishable from others in the region and hardly a match for its dignified neighbor, the historic city of Lille.[43] Roubaix was not a city whose artisanal manufacturing supported a regional population. Rather, "the factory created the city."[44]

The textile industry created Roubaix and dominated its economy from the 1820s when expansion began. Cotton mills first prompted the city's growth. In the 1830s Roubaix turned to wool, then expanded wool production to massive proportions with the use of mechanical wool combing.[45] By the end of the century, Roubaix was a factory city of 125,000, where workers supervised the milling, combing, and weaving of wool. These were the factories that feed our images of the Industrial Revolution, for the combing plants, which employed a quarter of the labor force, employed twelve to fifteen hundred workers. Wool mills and cloth production factories were smaller, yet each of them employed over one hundred workers by the end of the nineteenth century.[46] Here urbanization and industrialization went hand in hand; consequently, Roubaix provides a view of the emerging modern city more in keeping with our stereotypes than either Nîmes or Amiens. By its own historian the city was dubbed the "Manchester of France."[47]

The energy of an enterprising bourgeoisie fired the growth of factory industry. The family dynasties of the city were devoted not only to work but to diversification and growth of production as well—so much so that they were called the "Americans" of France.[48] It was not the

[43] Louis Trenard, *Histoire d'une métropole: Lille, Roubaix, Tourcoing* (Toulouse: Privat, 1977), pp. 33, 34, 54, 317.

[44] Ibid., p. 361.

[45] Georges Franchomme, "L'évolution démographique et économique de Roubaix dans le dernier tiers du XIXe siècle," *Revue du Nord* 51 (1969): 224; Trenard, *Histoire d'une métropole*, p. 322.

[46] Franchomme, "Roubaix," pp. 233–34; Michel Raman, "Mésure de la croissance d'un centre textile: Roubaix de 1789 à 1913," *Revue d'histoire économique et sociale* 51 (1973): 492.

[47] Théodore Leuridan, *Histoire de la fabrique de Roubaix* (Roubaix: Veuve Beghin, 1864), pp. 156–157, quoted in Louise Tilly, "Occupational Structure, Women's Work, and Demographic Change in Two French Industrial Cities, Anzin and Roubaix, 1872–1906," in *Time, Space and Man: Essays on Microdemography*, ed. Jan Sundin and Erik Soderlund (Atlantic Highlands, N.J.: Humanities Press, 1979), p. 112.

[48] David Landes, "Religion and Enterprise: The Case of the French Textile Indus-

Protestant ethic that prodded these captains of industry, for the bourgeoisie of Roubaix was composed of devout Catholics.[49] Likewise, the
city's workers were among the most religious in France. The histor-
ically devout "Vendée of the North" sent workers from just south of the
city and French Flanders sent workers from the west. The majority,
however, came from Belgium.[50]

Indeed, Belgians outnumbered French in Roubaix until the 1890s.[51]
In 1906 eight migrants in ten were from Belgium and the area immediately surrounding the city. Poverty and misery caused by the decline
of Belgium's rural linen industry pushed Belgians into France en masse
beginning in the 1840s. The ancient linen industry together with agriculture had supported the dense population of Belgium, but mechanical spinning and weaving produced a superior and cheaper product.
With the decline in demand for linen, many Belgians were forced to
seek work in the city.[52] This situation is similar to that in rural Picardy,
where crises in rural cloth production pushed people off the land. Yet
unlike the rural people who moved to Amiens, the Belgians in Roubaix
formed a community apart, defined by religious culture, economic specialization, and language. The Bishop of Ghent in Belgium, for example, assigned Flemish-speaking priests to Roubaix for the many
Belgians who spoke neither French nor its Flemish dialect.[53] Belgians
remained attached to home. Part of this attachment was practical, because naturalization to French citizenship was beyond workers' bud-
gets. Moreover, the industrial crises that periodically shook Roubaix
made it necessary for Belgians to return home when they were unem-
ployed where living costs were lower. Finally, naturalized citizens

---

try," in *Enterprise and Entrepreneurs in Nineteenth- and Twentieth-Century France*,
ed. Edward C. Carter II, Robert Forster, and Joseph N. Moody (Baltimore, Md.: Johns
Hopkins University Press, 1976), p. 43.

[49]Claude Fohlen, *L'industrie textile au temps du Second Empire* (Paris: Plon, 1956),
pp. 82–88; David Landes, "Religion and Enterprise," pp. 43–78; Bonnie G. Smith,
*Ladies of the Leisure Class: The Bourgeoises of Northern France in the Nineteenth Cen-
tury* (Princeton, N.J.: Princeton University Press, 1981).

[50]Yves-Marie Hilaire, "Les ouvriers de la région du Nord devant l'Eglise catholique
(XIXe et XXe siècles)," *Mouvement Social* 57 (1966): 190.

[51]Franchomme, "Roubaix," p. 210.

[52]Fermin Lentacker, *La frontière franco-belge: étude géographique des effets d'une
frontière internationale sur la vie des relations* (Lille: Morel and Corduant, 1974), pp.
221–23; Vandervelde, *L'exode rural*, p. 84.

[53]Franchomme, "Roubaix," pp. 211–12.

were subject in France to compulsory military service—utterly unknown in Belgium until World War I.[54]

Most Belgians, therefore, retained their status as foreign workers, taking advantage of the relatively high wages and availability of jobs in France by crossing the border and moving five miles to Roubaix. With time, in fact, it became less necessary to live in France because Roubaix spread toward the border and transportation improved. As a consequence, up to 40,000 Belgians commuted daily or weekly to the city in 1905—by train, tram, bicycle, or on foot.[55] Permanent or temporary residents, the Belgian workers with their religious convictions put a distinctive stamp on the city.

So did its unbridled growth. As Roubaix more than tripled in size between 1851 and 1901, it had no old city to preserve, no city walls to transgress, and no outlying areas to fill in. Rather, it formed satellite cities and sprawled over the fields. It was the quintessential "tentacular city," in the words of one poet, a city that sent out rail lines like antennae and pulled in the goods and people of the countryside.[56] Because Roubaix grew so quickly and to such a large size, workers' housing was in short supply. An entrepreneur complained to his son in the 1850s that workers were scarce because housing could not be found: "There is not one available dwelling. Houses are inhabited before they are finished, before the stairway is installed. The inhabitants climb a ladder like chickens going to roost under the roof to go to bed."[57] As factories grew, the need for housing expanded. And as the great entrepreneurs invested in factories, housing was left to members of the middle class looking for profit from a relatively modest investment. A quite horrible form of housing unique to the area emerged as a result. Called the *courée*, this housing put the most dwellings possible on the

---

[54]Noëlle Dombrowski-Kéerle, "Le divorce dans le Nord de 1884 à 1914 (Aspects démographiques et sociaux, étude statistique)," in *L'homme, la vie et la mort dans le Nord au 19e siècle*, ed. Marcel Gillet (Lille: Editions Universitaires, 1972), p. 192; G. Eeckhout, "Les ouviers belges dans le Nord," *Revue sociale catholique* (June, 1900): 273; Franchomme, "Roubaix," p. 211; Reybaud, *La laine*, pp. 212–13.

[55]Great Britain, Board of Trade, *Cost of Living in French Towns*, p. 276; Lentacker, *Le frontière franco-belge*, p. 267; Jacques Prouvost, "Les courées à Roubaix," *Revue du Nord* 51 (April–June, 1969): 312; Trenard, *Histoire d'une métropole*, p. 362.

[56]Vandervelde, *L'exode rural*, p. 19; Emile Verhaeren, *Les villes tentaculaires* (Paris: Mercure de France, 1904).

[57]Prouvost, "Les courées," p. 313.

least terrain in the cheapest fashion. Since street-front property was expensive, developers bought deep narrow pieces. Along such corridors, each perhaps seventy feet across and five hundred feet deep, row houses would be built perpendicular to the street, and between the houses would stretch a narrow dark pathway serving up to forty houses. A shelter at the end protected common toilets and a water pump. Cabarets often occupied the large front building. *Courées* and similar housing provided shelter for workers throughout Roubaix's history, but they nearly doubled in number in the decade after 1896. Forty percent of the city's workers probably lived in such dwellings in 1906.[58]

The horror of this particular housing lay in its effects on physical health. Because the narrow houses were built without space between or behind them, the only light and air came from front windows, and the lack of fresh air encouraged tuberculosis and helped maintain an extraordinarily high rate of infant mortality in Roubaix throughout the nineteenth century. Crowded living in the *courées* doubtless fostered the high crime and juvenile delinquency of the city.[59]

The moral and physical well-being of the family was the greatest concern of the day. Although we have no workers' accounts of their conditions, a family history written by a working-class woman born in the 1920s confirms that physical deprivation, ill health, and angry social relations were exacerbated by the city's crowded and unsanitary housing.[60] For one contemporary observer of Roubaix, the quality of working-class lives "was strictly tied with the quality of their housing," and large families suffered most because they lived in more crowded quarters.[61] "This misery offends not only the senses," wrote another in the 1860s, "it also wounds modesty."[62] Consequently, private charity in Roubaix distributed bedding as one of its major contributions to the

---

[58] Ibid., pp. 307, 311, 315.

[59] Eeckhout, "Les ouvriers belges," p. 272; Aline Lesaege-Dugied, "La mortalité infantile dans le département du Nord," in *L'homme, la vie et la mort dans le Nord au 19e siècle*, ed. Marcel Gillet (Lille: Editions Universitaires, 1972), pp. 85–89; Prouvost, "Les courées," p. 316.

[60] Madame G. [name disguised by an initial] (Unpublished manuscript, Roubaix, 1962); see Louise Tilly's essay in this volume.

[61] Paul Descamps, "La Flandre française: L'ouvrier de l'industrie textile," *La science sociale* 42, no. 59 (June, 1900): 88.

[62] Reybaud, *Le coton*, p. 230.

poor family: mattresses, covers, and curtains to separate male and female adolescents.[63]

The factory gave rise to a moral concern because it was perceived as the cause of consensual unions and the illegitimate children resulting from such unions. In the textile mill, scantily clad men and women worked in a humid, warm atmosphere. "When the threshold of the factory is crossed," asked Audiganne, "who can prevent the consequences of the relationships formed there?"[64] The community, replied Reybaud nearly a decade later; he accounted for a low rate of illegitimacy by the strength of community opinion and religious belief, particularly among the city's Belgians.[65] By the turn of the century, the proportion of illegitimate children produced by Belgians in Roubaix was higher than at home in Belgium, partly because they lacked both the civil status documents required to marry in France and the fees for marriage. Their energy was spent on labor and their earnings on groceries and rent. Despite this, the Belgians probably had fewer illegitimate children than the native-born French and certainly fewer than the workers of Amiens. They rarely divorced and were much less likely to do so than workers in Amiens.[66]

Nonetheless, the church expressed great concern for the working family and the Belgian family. Clerics complained that "industry leads to the regression of Christian habits," and even stated baldly that "industry kills souls."[67] Workers were being reduced to cogwheels appended to their machines: voluntary and intelligent cogs, in the words of Canon Fichaux, but cogs nevertheless.[68]

A devout and patriarchal bourgeoisie mobilized to protect the working-class family, and the zeal with which it did so sets Roubaix apart. Religion increasingly entered the factory between 1850 and

[63] Ibid.

[64] Audiganne, *Les populations ouvrières*, p. 14.

[65] Reybaud, *La laine*, p. 212.

[66] Claude Hélène Dewaepenaere, "L'enfance illegitime dans le département du Nord au XIXe siècle," in *L'homme, la vie et la mort dans le Nord au 19e siècle*, ed. Marcel Gillet (Lille: Editions Universitaires, 1972), pp. 151–53; Dombrowski-Kéerle, "Le divorce dans le Nord," pp. 185–86; Etienne van de Walle, *The Female Population of France in the Nineteenth Century* (Princeton: Princeton University Press, 1974), pp. 394, 440.

[67] Quoted in Hilaire, "Les ouvriers," p. 192.

[68] Franchomme, "Roubaix," p. 223.

1914. Employers encouraged prayers in the work place, cults with names like "Our Lady of the Factory," statues of the Virgin in offices and shops, the use of nuns as moral supervisors in the women's workrooms, gifts to children on communion, classes on catechism for the children, and time off for services. All of these were part of factory life under the devout bourgeoisie of Roubaix. In fact, workers complained about the prominent role of religion in the mill.[69]

The family focus of the bourgeoisie of Roubaix expressed itself most clearly in women's charities in which aid to expectant mothers and to families with insufficient beds depended on the recipient's proof of her good character and marital status: "Though poverty was negotiable, virtue and religion were not."[70] In the good cause of advancing motherhood for the poor with layettes, midwives' fees, and paid time off, the bourgeoisie of Roubaix had no intention of allowing it to be "blemished by encouragement for the slovenly, unchaste, or wanton women" of the city.[71] Likewise, some of the most active charities of the area had the goal of the Society of Saint François de Régis in Lille: to promote marriages and the legitimization of children by procuring the required documents and fees for marriage.[72]

Urban Families and the Migrant

As different as Roubaix may have been from Amiens and Nîmes to the south, all three cities exemplify the trend of urbanization, which accelerated on the continent between 1850 and the First World War. Each city grew by at least half and did so at the expense of the surrounding countryside.[73] In the process, each was associated with the rural exodus decimating rural France and Belgium as people sought steady work in the city. City growth aroused concern over the family of the migrant worker. In the case of Amiens, the family of the rural weaver was most worrisome; in Nîmes, the rural peasant family. Those in Roubaix focused on the Belgian worker's family.

---

[69] Hilaire, "Les ouvriers," p. 192; Landes, "Religion and Enterprise," p. 77.
[70] Smith, *Ladies of the Leisure Class*, p. 139.
[71] Ibid., p. 140.
[72] Audiganne, *Les populations ouvrières*, pp. 13–15.
[73] Between 1851 and 1901, Amiens grew by 80 percent, Nîmes by 70 percent, and Roubaix by 237 percent.

Was this concern warranted? Workers' diaries do not tell us, for the shops and factories of the *Belle Epoque* allowed workers little time for education or for reflection, so historians have few diaries or memoirs from the working class. Yet their family lives are traced in their living patterns and in the evolution of these patterns for the young, newly arrived migrants, for the middle-aged worker, and for the elderly. These patterns were recorded for native and migrant alike in the census lists of Amiens, Nîmes, and Roubaix in 1906, lists that give the origins of each city dweller and organize citizens by household, specifying their relationships with one another. Consequently, the historian can compare the family living patterns of migrants in the three cities.[74] The census is a slender resource for the historian. But if close attention is paid to the patterns it reveals and an eye is kept to literature and contemporary studies, some insight may be gained into the family of the migrant and by extension into the urban family of the early twentieth century.

"Those who leave their native area," observed a Picard scholar in 1905, "are the young people who procreate and who form families. The village keeps the old ones."[75] He could have been describing any area of the Western world, because it was typically young people who sought their fortunes in the city. The large proportion of newcomers under the age of thirty in all three of the cities under investigation here suggests that the cities fit the international tendency to attract the young.[76]

The initial experience for the newcomer was often not a family experience. (See Table 1.) The census shows that young men and some young women lived in a rented room as lodgers or with the family for which they worked. This was true particularly in Nîmes, where one young man in four resided in such a situation. (Young migrants are defined as those aged fifteen to twenty-nine.) Yet this hardly spelled isolation, for the rented room was usually *en garni*, a French arrangement for room rental and meals in a particular establishment. The people in

[74] Information on individual migrants in the three cities comes from a systematic sample of inhabitants in every tenth household in Amiens and Roubaix and of every twentieth household in Nîmes. (Sample drawn from the 1906 census lists.)

[75] Demangeon, *La Picardie*, p. 407.

[76] Between 26 percent and 37 percent of the migrants in Amiens, Nîmes, and Roubaix were under the age of thirty. The proportion of migrant women under thirty was greater than that of migrant men under thirty.

TABLE 1. Household Position of Migrants Aged 15 to 29 in Amiens, Nîmes, and Roubaix, by Sex, 1906

Migrants	Solitary	House-hold Head	Spouse	Child	Lodg-er	Servant	Other Rela-tive	Non-rela-tive	Total	N
Males										
Amiens	6%	36%	NA	40%	2%	4%	6%	5%	99%	343
Nîmes	10	25	NA	44	6	7	7	2	101	117
Roubaix	9	30	NA	47	4	2	5	3	100	371
Females										
Amiens	4	2	40	24	2	19	6	3	100	503
Nîmes	3	3	28	25	3	29	8	3	102	240
Roubaix	4	2	31	35	2	17	6	2	99	567

NOTE: NA, category not applicable.

the rooms ate in the same restaurant and often worked together as well. Small spaces and shared facilities added to the intimacy of the *garni*, as the story of Jean-Baptiste Larencontre's first days in Roubaix indicates: he was shown by a fellow worker to a suitable *garni* over a cabaret fronting one of the *courées*. Larencontre lived in a room measuring eight feet square, but he took his meals in the café below and mixed with the people in the *courée* because he shared their water pump and toilet. Soon, in the public intimacy of this living arrangement, he knew everyone.[77]

Young women were even more likely than men to live apart from their families, because a great many were domestic servants. In Amiens and Nîmes, this experience was common for women from the immediate area and region around the city. For example, Juliette Sauget and her two sisters, daughters of an agricultural laborer in the Somme, all worked as domestics in Amiens about 1906. Over a third of the young women in Nîmes from the region worked as servants. Service was important even in Roubaix where the bourgeoisie vied with the factory for the services of young women. There young Belgians were

[77] Jacques Marseille, *Une famille d'ouvriers de 1770 à nos jours* (Paris: Hachette, 1981), pp. 102–103.

the servants—not those from border towns, but from distant rural areas.[78] Into the twentieth century, then, and even in a factory town, domestic service was an important employment for rural women who sought an avenue into the city and a roof over their heads. Even these women, living in an attic and apart from their own families, may have been less isolated than the census indicates. They may have had relatives or compatriots in town. In her memoir, Juliette Sauget explains that she went to Amiens because she had sisters there who could help her. A case study of country women in Nîmes has unearthed a wealth of ties among sisters in the city. Often their urban history begins with an elder sister's initial employment as a servant, then her marriage, and the procession of younger sisters to town to take up the tradition.[79]

Some young migrants were already married. Migrants married earliest in Amiens, apparently. Nearly a quarter of the migrant young men and a third of the young women were married before the age of thirty. (The proportion is smaller among migrants in Nîmes and Roubaix.) More still lived with their parents: a quarter of the young men, about 40 percent of the young women, and, not unexpectedly, nearly all those under the age of fifteen did so. This is a good indication that many families were moving together to Amiens, Nîmes, and Roubaix. Yet historians have focused so intently on young single migrants that they have underestimated how many families were on the road in urbanizing Europe. Like one family from the Cévennes mountains, many families appear to have arrived together in the city. In that case, the father worked in the wool industry and came to the city when it

[78] Marthe-Juliette Mouillon, "Un exemple de migration rurale: De la Somme dans la capitale. Domestique de la Belle Epoque à Paris (1904–1912)," *Etudes de la région parisienne* 44, no. 27 (July, 1970): 1–9. Of the female migrants aged fifteen to twenty-nine, 20 percent of those in Amiens from the region worked as domestic servants; 31 percent of those in Nîmes from within a twenty-kilometer radius and 34 percent from the region worked as domestic servants; and 28 percent of those in Roubaix from Belgium beyond a twenty-kilometer radius worked as domestic servants.

[79] Abel Chatelain, "Migrations et domesticité féminine urbaine en France, XVIII siècle–XXe siècle," *Revue d'histoire économique et sociale* 47 (1960): 506–28; Theresa McBride, *The Domestic Revolution: The Modernisation of Household Service in England and France, 1820–1920* (New York: Holmes and Meier, 1976), chapter 4; Leslie Page Moch, "Domestic Service in Paris: An Avenue into the City" (Unpublished manuscript, University of Michigan, 1974); Moch, *Paths to the City*, chap. 4; Mouillon, "Un exemple de migration rurale," pp. 5–7; Louise A. Tilly and Joan W. Scott, *Women, Work and Family* (New York: Holt, Rinehart and Winston, 1978), pp. 34–37, 107–10.

TABLE 2. Occupations of Employed Migrants Residing with Parents
in Amiens, Nîmes, and Roubaix, 1906

Migrants	Leather	Gar-ment	Tex-tile	Other	Trans-port	Com-merce	Admin/Prof/Bourg	Ser-vant	B.C.Ser-vice	Total	N
Males											
Amiens	6%	2%	16%	30%	3%	30%	3%	3%	6%	99%	122
Nîmes	16	6	NA	19	0	38	13	3	6	101	32
Roubaix	NA	NA	53	27	16	NA	1	3	NA	100	189
Females											
Amiens	1	40	20	13	—	12	5	8	—	99	85
Nîmes	0	69	NA	3	3	14	3	6	3	101	35
Roubaix	NA	NA	51	34	9	—	4	2	NA	100	163

NOTE: NA, no comparable category in analysis of the labor force; —, less than 0.5 percent. "Admin/Prof/Bourg" includes administrators, professionals, and the bourgeoisie. Blue collar (b.c.) service includes housekeepers, laundresses, concièrges, gardeners, and hairdressers.

failed. His wages as a day laborer in Nîmes in combination with those of his three seamstress daughters supported the family. The family stayed together in order to work and combine their wages.[80]

This was particularly true for families who moved to Roubaix, for there over a third of the young migrant women and nearly half the men lived with their parents. (See Table 1.) Moreover, they were more likely to be employed than the children of migrants in Amiens and Nîmes. According to our understanding of wages and prices in that city, as recorded by the British Board of Trade, it was necessary to have several members working in order to keep a family fed. Half the working children were employed in the textile industry, like Victorine Henneton who lived with her parents and worked in a weaving mill.[81] (See Table 2.) Others were laundresses, seamstresses, and construction workers. Factory employment was particularly attractive to migrating families.

The configuration of employment in migrant families was quite dif-

[80] Leslie Page Moch, "Marriage, Migration and Urban Demographic Structure: A Case from France in the Belle Epoque," *Journal of Family History* 6, no. 1 (Spring, 1981): 70–88; Moch, *Paths to the City,* chap. 4.

[81] Marseille, *Une famille d'ouvriers,* pp. 103–105; Tilly and Dubnoff, "Families and Wage Earning," p. 6.

ferent in Amiens and Nîmes. Young men who lived with their parents
in Amiens worked in textiles or in the shoe industry, and in both towns
they worked in the city's various smaller industries. Women like the
mountain-born sisters in Nîmes sewed for a living. But in addition to
those performing industrial work, a large proportion worked in commerce—as clerks, office workers, or as sales people. Most of these
white-collar jobs required more education and commanded more respect than industrial jobs. In the words of one female factory worker,
"Me, at ease in front of a sales girl? . . . A salesgirl, that's someone
infinitely superior, a girl who wasn't sent into the factory at the age of
twelve, who learned to carry herself, to speak well. When she leaves
the store, she is an elegant *demoiselle* who looks down on workers in
the street."[82] The white-collar job, especially a secure government job,
was the goal of many young people at the turn of the century. But to
obtain such a position, the family had to be able to forego the children's
wages during their years of education and training. Consequently, the
commercial workers who lived with their parents in Amiens and Nîmes
reflect the presence of parents who were able to support them (and
who were themselves often white-collar workers). Thus the prosperous
or ambitious families from small towns in Picardy and in Languedoc
came to the regional capital where their children were educated for
white-collar work. A joiner's son from the mountains of Languedoc, for
example, married a schoolteacher and brought his family to Nîmes
when he secured an administrative post at the prefecture. His son
went into administration after completing his education.[83] In Amiens,
the young men whose families supported their entry into commerce
came not from the immediate area, but from the region at large and
the rest of France. Some were part of the colony of outsiders referred
to above who worked in the bureaucracy. In Nîmes, young white-collar
workers were from the region. And they were likely to be Protestants:
the aspirations of the Cevenol focused on white-collar work at the turn
of the century.[84] A study of young migrants in Nîmes shows that those
from the Protestant Cévennes often arrived with their families and
went to school or obtained white-collar jobs and those from the Catho-

[82] Marseille, *Une famille d'ouvriers*, p. 105.
[83] Moch, *Paths to the City*, chap. 1.
[84] Michael Roussy, "Evolution démographique et économique des populations du
Gard" (Thèse du droit, Université de Montpellier, 1949), pp. 69–70.

lic Lozère worked for the railroad or at less skilled jobs and lived in *garnis* or as domestic servants.[85]

On the whole, the young migrants' initial urban experience was not a family one. Like the young men in Amiens, the men in *garnis* in Nîmes, and the servants in all three cities, the most common experience was to leave home and family. If reformers' concern focused on any group, it was on these highly visible young newcomers who were not with their families—the men who were susceptible to evenings in the cabaret and fights that often resulted and the women who were vulnerable to seduction, abandonment, and resulting illegitimate children.[86] For example, an article in a 1906 Nîmes newspaper relates the story of a domestic servant from a mountain village who set up housekeeping with a worker on the basis of his promise of marriage—a promise not offered seriously, as she discovered when he returned to his regular post, wife, and family in a nearby town. The enraged young woman then appeared at her former lover's place of employment and berated him with such vigor that the police intervened on his behalf.[87]

Historians are beginning to understand that the experience of seduction and abandonment or the consensual union that produced illegitimate children was regarded as a failure by the women involved, a failure resulting from their lack of power and economic viability in the city. Local evidence from Amiens suggests that migrant women were likely to bear the city's illegitimate children: in 1851 they bore half the illegitimate children, but were less than 40 percent of the city's brides.[88] More general evidence suggests that the community's ability to promote marriage once pregnancy occurs is the crucial element preventing illegitimate births. Migrant women were particularly vulnerable, then, because that supportive community was not in place for them as it would have been in their home village or small town.[89] Con-

[85] Leslie Page Moch, "Adolescence and Migration to Nîmes, 1906," *Social Science History* 5 (1981): 25–51.

[86] Descamps, "La Flandre française," pp. 60–61.

[87] *Petit Républicain du Midi (Nîmes)*, July 21, 1906.

[88] Michel Frey, "Du mariage et du concubinage dans les classes populaires à Paris (1846–1847)," *Annales: Economies, Sociétés, Civilisations* 33 (1978): 803–29; Litchfield and Gordon, "Closing the 'Tour,'" p. 462.

[89] Louise A. Tilly, Joan W. Scott, and Miriam Cohen, "Women's Work and European Fertility Patterns," *Journal of Interdisciplinary History* 6 (1976): 447–76. Archives of the Tribunal at Nîmes, marriage records, 1906, record the legitimization of children at their

TABLE 3. Household Position of Migrants Aged 30 to 59 in Amiens, Nîmes, and Roubaix, by Sex, 1906

Migrants	Solitary	House-hold Head	Spouse	Child	Lodg-er	Servant	Other Rela-tive	Non-rela-tive	Total	N
Males, aged 30–44										
Amiens	5%	87%	NA	3%	1%	2%	1%	1%	100%	522
Nîmes	8	85	NA	3	1	1	2	1	101	211
Roubaix	9	82	NA	4	3	—	2	0	100	549
Females, aged 30–44										
Amiens	4	8	72	4	1	7	3	2	101	583
Nîmes	3	11	68	4	—	9	4	2	101	263
Roubaix	5	8	75	4	1	5	3	1	102	533
Males, aged 45–59										
Amiens	6	88	NA	1	1	2	2	1	101	389
Nîmes	7	88	NA	1	0	0	3	1	100	165
Roubaix	13	80	NA	1	3	0	3	—	100	439
Females, aged 45–59										
Amiens	8	13	61	1	1	8	8	1	101	43
Nîmes	7	20	64	1	0	3	5	1	101	17
Roubaix	5	16	71	1	1	3	3	—	100	46

NOTE: NA, category not applicable; —, less than 0.5 percent.

sensual unions were in many cases long lasting and stable, eventually resulting in marriage.[90]

According to the census, migrants did marry. In Amiens, Nîmes, and Roubaix, the vast majority succeeded in marrying by their middle years (here defined as ages thirty to forty-four), for about eight in ten men and seven in ten women in 1906 reported themselves as living with a spouse. Some men and women did live alone or as servants, but these are only a few. (See Table 3.) And a minority of migrant women— a group that increased as they grew older—headed their own households. But like Larencontre, who married a woman from the *courée*

---

parents' marriage and report the starting date of the parents' consensual union. This is true of all French marriage records of the period.

[90] Lenard Berlanstein, "Illegitimacy, Concubinage, and Proletarianization in a French Rural Town, 1760–1914," *Journal of Family History* 5, no. 4 (1980): p. 360; Frey, "Du mariage et du concubinage."

behind his rented room, most migrants found a spouse in the city. Life stories drawn from marriage and birth records corroborate the patterns, suggested by the census lists, of meeting and marriage after arrival in the city. A peasant's son, for example, came to work for the railroad in Nîmes and soon married the daughter of a co-worker from the mountains. Juliette Sauget moved on from Amiens to become a domestic in Paris, where she eventually worked as a nurse and married; two of her sisters who were domestics in Amiens married and settled there.[91]

Cities in urbanizing Europe were the meeting ground for young men and women. But because men and women rarely worked together, they did not meet in the workshop. Rather they met through friends and relatives, like the peasant's son met his bride, or because they lived close together, like Larencontre and his bride, who were residents of the same *courée* in Roubaix. Young people also met at Sunday café concerts and bandstand concerts in Amiens and Nîmes and at public dances on July fourteenth and other festive occasions. Boulevards and parks provided a chance to see and be seen on Sunday, when young men and women would parade before each other. For most migrants between the ages of thirty and fifty-nine, marriage and an urban family resulted. Migrant men and women in many cases were just as likely to marry, if not more so, than natives of Amiens, Nîmes, or Roubaix. (See Table 4.) This was particularly true in Nîmes, where natives of the city often remained single.[92]

Many marriages remained intact as migrants entered their sixties, yet for both the migrant and native over sixty years of age, widowhood took its toll. (See Table 5.) As men and women lost their spouses they appeared in the census as single heads of their own households. Also, many elderly men and a significant proportion of women resided with their grown children. This suggests that some elderly, particularly women, may have migrated to town after they were widowed to be with their children. Parents might have continued in the family enterprise when their youthful children moved to the city, but at the death of a spouse the widow or widower abandoned the home and joined the children.

A case study gives a concrete idea of how this migration worked:

[91] Mouillon, "Un exemple de migration rurale," p. 8.
[92] Moch, "Marriage, Migration and Urban Demographic Structure."

TABLE 4. Proportion Currently Married Aged 30 to 44 in Amiens, Nîmes, and Roubaux, by Sex and Origin, 1906

Group	Native-born Urban Dwellers	Migrants
Males		
Amiens	80%	82%
Nîmes	70	82
Roubaix	78	77
Females		
Amiens	75	70
Nîmes	62	70
Roubaix	75	73

TABLE 5. Household Position of Migrants Aged 60 and Over in Amiens, Nîmes, and Roubaix, by Sex, 1906

Migrants	Solitary	House-hold Head	Spouse	Child	Lodg-er	Ser-vant	Other Rela-tive	Non-rela-tive	Total	N
Males										
Amiens	10%	77%	NA	0	2%	1%	10%	1%	101%	188
Nîmes	7	76	NA	0	1	1	13	1	99	97
Roubaix	12	77	NA	—	3	—	7	0	99	241
Females										
Amiens	16	19	29	1%	1	5	28	2	101	277
Nîmes	7	28	22	0	0	1	39	3	100	98
Roubaix	11	27	39	0	2	1	21	0	101	263

NOTE: NA, category not applicable; —, less than 0.5 percent.

François Moulin had remained in a small mountain town when his daughter Anna became a servant in Nîmes. When Anna married a tramway worker from a peasant village not far from their own, the Moulins came to town for the wedding, but returned home where Monsieur Moulin continued to earn his living as a baker. Several years later, after his wife had died and he was sixty-four years of age, old Moulin resided in Nîmes with Anna, and his two other daughters worked in the city as domestic servants.[93] Such a pattern was less prevalent in Roubaix, where fewer elderly women and men lived with children and other relatives. It is likely that the entire family—not simply the young—originally had migrated together, attracted by factory employment.

Conclusion

The contrast between the concerns of urban reformers and the actual living situation of migrants indicates at which points nineteenth-century reformers and today's historians are not speaking to the same issues. Few of the sources, like the census lists that are currently explored for information about the urban family, address the concerns of unhealthy housing, alcohol consumption, or rates of illegitimacy.[94] An analysis of living patterns gives little support for the notion that the migrant was lost in familial terms. On the contrary, young migrants lived in close proximity with others, if not with their own family, and their formation of close ties is reflected in the high proportion who eventually entered conjugal relationships. This was the case especially in Nîmes, where migrants were more likely to marry than the middle-class natives who delayed marriage in deference to education, training, or financial security.[95] In Amiens and Roubaix, migrant women's marriage patterns were close to those of native-born city women. Migrants in Roubaix were particularly likely to reside with their families.

This does not mean that we can dismiss reformers' concerns. Many were warranted, particularly concerns with housing, which working-class memoirs as well as reformers' observations described as unhealthy and demoralizing. The difference between the two perceptions is that memoirs catalog the survival of the stable family despite its miserable physical environment, while the observations of reformers do not. The memoir of artisan Paul Marcelin from Nîmes describes his family's uncomfortable and unsanitary housing, the deaths of his six

[93] Moch, *Paths to the City*, chap. 2.

[94] Historians of demographic patterns, however, do investigate illegitimacy: Litchfield and Gordon's "Closing of the 'Tour'" is one such investigation; see also Peter Laslett, *Family Life and Illicit Love in Earlier Generations* (Cambridge: Cambridge University Press, 1977).

[95] See Frey, "Du mariage et du concubinage," and Moch, "Marriage, Migration and Urban Demographic Structure."

siblings (five with a rural wet nurse), and the ceaseless work of his united family. According to Marcelin, life in Nîmes was really very difficult—"mediocre, if not miserable salaries, frequent unemployment, uncomfortable housing, so many trials to overcome."[96] This may be the most accurate assessment of urban working-class life, particularly for the newcomer.

If reformers were sensitive to the trials of urban life, they were less aware of the human relationships that helped urban working-class people to survive. Recent research focuses on these relationships, and herein lies its value. Reconstructing networks of kin and friendship from census lists and other documents reveals the means by which the difficulties of urban life were overcome by people who had few other resources. The solidarity of family and friends was virtually ignored, for example, by reformers concerned with working-class housing. Observers' eyes invariably came to rest on the mattress shared by several family members: incest was a secondary but constant theme of writing on working-class housing. Yet in workers' eyes the shared bed inspired the quite different sentiment of caring for sick children. Likewise, concern with alcoholism among workers was warranted, but it was fallacious to conclude that moral degeneracy was at the base of alcoholism or illegitimacy. Reformers have provided us with invaluable observations of urban life, but because they viewed it through the distorting prism of nineteenth-century moralism, their explanations and analyses are less valuable to the historian.

This study of families in three expanding cities has highlighted the importance of migration in family groups, particularly in response to factory employment in Roubaix. Roubaix's relatively successful industry could employ several members of the family, but in Amiens and Nîmes there were fewer opportunities for family employment. There young people were more employable than their parents were. The young were more likely to have the training for clerical jobs, to be strong enough for railroad work, or to be acceptable as domestic servants. Consequently, young people came to commercial and administrative centers like Amiens and Nîmes without their parents. If their parents did come, they were themselves white-collar workers or unskilled workers displaced by age or economic change, such as the day

[96] Marcelin, *Souvenirs*, p. 28.

laborer from the mountains who was formerly a wool worker. Some parents joined migrants at the end of their own working lives. Thus kin were important to migrants in all three cities, but the factory city in particular enabled families to move together, live together, and find employment for several family members.

In both factory town and commercial or administrative center, the newcomers who stayed on into their middle years married and formed urban families. In that way the migrants' life cycle reflects the broad shift to permanent settlement in an urban area.[97] Domestic service or urban labor became an entry into permanent urban residence. The founding of urban families by thousands of French raised in villages and small towns signaled the trend to permanent settlement. Thus, the decision to form an urban family is at the heart of the process of urbanization. The family was not destroyed by the city in turn-of-the-century France; rather, the family created and expanded the city.

[97] For a theoretical overview, see Charles Tilly, "Migration in Modern European History," in *Human Migration, Patterns and Policies*, ed. William McNeill and Ruth Adams (Bloomington: Indiana University Press, 1978). For examples, see Abel Chatelain, *Les migrants temporaires en France de 1800 à 1914* (Lille: Presses Universitaires de Lille, 1976); John Gillis, *Youth and History: Tradition and Change in European Age Relations* (New York: Academic Press, 1974); and Yves Lequin, *Les ouvriers de la région lyonnaise* (Lyon: Presses Universitaires de Lyon, 1977).

LOUISE A. TILLY

Rich and Poor in a
French Textile City

BOTH an elegant boulevard and a streetcar line run from the great commercial city Lille to its textile satellite Roubaix. The boulevard runs beside an artfully natural park, designed at the turn of the twentieth century. Dignified, spacious houses of the city's manufacturers and entrepreneurs line the street. Continuing into the heart of Roubaix, a visitor finds the handsome, massive city hall facing its symmetrical twin, the chamber of commerce building, across the city's main square.

One block away begin the factories: smoke-blackened red brick buildings ranging in style from industrial Gothic to utilitarian shed. Streetcars stop at factory gates. Right off the main street, a visitor can turn into a *courée*, the typical working-class housing of another era. Most Americans must duck their heads to pass through the low archway into the narrow, littered courtyard.

What a difference between the physical surroundings of rich and poor! The textile industry, source of wealth for entrepreneurs and of livelihood for workers, joins the two neighborhoods. But the difference between wealth and livelihood separates them. In many respects, the neighborhoods are worlds apart. They meet only at work.

What of the families in these worlds? How did industrialism affect them, and how did they respond to it? Sociologist William J. Goode has offered a hypothesis about the "fit" of the conjugal family and industrialism that posits critical class differences: "The middle and upper strata are by definition more 'successful' in the obvious sense that they own [industry], dominate it, occupy its highest positions, and direct its future. . . . The upper strata recognize the widest extension of kin,

My thanks to Charles Tilly for his comments. A grant from the American Philosophical Society and a fellowship from the Shelby Cullom Davis Center for Historical Study made possible the early stages of this research.

maintain most control over the courtship and marriage choices of their young, and are most likely to give and receive help from one another."[1] Goode's hypothesis claims that upper-class families, in addition to their access to powerful economic resources, can mobilize an extended kin network to promote or defend family interest. In contrast, "the lower-class family is indeed most 'integrated' with the industrial system but mainly in the sense that the individual is forced to enter its labor market with far less family support—his family *does not prevent industry from using him for its own goals* . . . lower-strata families are most likely to be 'conjugal' and to serve the needs of the industrial system."[2] Goode concludes, then, that because lower-class families lack the economic resources and kin networks of the wealthy they are in double jeopardy in relation to the industrial economy.

Contrary to this hypothesis, both historical and contemporary studies have shown that working-class families are not completely without kin networks.[3] Further, even in the absence of extended kin, the conjugal family and household are sources of material assistance to individuals in industrialized settings.[4] The family economy and family strategies of rich and poor in the industrial period are different, yet in both classes, families and individuals have been able to tap personal and collective resources in ways that Goode's hypothesis misses. Only close examination of specific historical cases can answer these questions: (1) To what extent were families, rich and poor, able to develop strategies to maintain or improve their position in society? (2) How did these strategies affect the behavior and areas of choice of individual members of these families?

[1] William J. Goode, *World Revolution and Family Patterns* (New York: The Free Press of Glenco, 1963), p. 12.

[2] Ibid., p. 13.

[3] See, for example, Tamara K. Hareven, "Family Time and Industrial Time: Family and Work in a Planned Corporation Town, 1900–1924," in *Family and Kin in Urban Communities, 1700–1930*, ed. Tamara Hareven (New York: Franklin Watts, 1977), pp. 187–207, and Michael Young and Peter Willmott, *Family and Kinship in East London* (New York: Penguin, 1957).

[4] Michael Anderson, *Family Structure in Nineteenth Century Lancashire* (Cambridge: Cambridge University Press, 1971), and Claudia Goldin, "Family Strategies and the Family Economy in the Late Nineteenth Century: The Role of Secondary Workers," in *Philadelphia: Work, Space, Family, and Group Experience in the Nineteenth Century*, ed. Theodore Herschberg (New York: Oxford University Press, 1981), pp. 277–310.

This essay is such a study. It compares the family economy and family strategies of rich and poor in Roubaix around 1900 on such matters as work, fertility, education, placement of sons and daughters, and family consumption patterns. The family economy is defined here as that arena of family life that links individual members with the economic system in which they live through allocation of resources and persons in economic roles, public and private. The concept of family strategies works as a series of hypotheses about the implicit principles, those less articulated than strict rules of decision making, that inform and shape family behavior. The household as a whole is the unit that defines family strategies; the goal of such strategies is the promotion of the good of the household.[5] Although families are conceived of as acting in a unitary way to make decisions about behavior, it is not argued that all family members benefit or lose equally from strategies or the outcomes based on them. Some individuals are constrained; others see their freedom of choice enhanced. Strategies are conceived of here as problematic and contingent; the creation of strategies is a process both of negotiation and struggle. Strategies are also subject to change. The disadvantages or advantages *systematically* accruing to individuals by virtue of their family position—husband, wife, daughter, son—are illuminated here.

The essay is organized in the following way: the first section examines the economic situation of Roubaix around 1900. The second section looks at patterns of family life in a group of wealthy families of the city, with emphasis on decisions about child rearing, marriage, work, and how kin networks affect such decisions. The third section turns to working-class families and their way of life, examining the patterns of behavior that suggest family strategies about reproduction, schooling, occupation, and consumption. The fourth section takes the Roubaix working-class family outside the private arena and into organizational life and collective action. It shows how class-based activity may be conceived of as an extension of family strategies, in its concern with the

[5] Pierre Bourdieu, "Marriage Strategies as Strategies of Social Reproduction," in *Family and Society, Selections from the Annales: Economies, Sociétés, Civilisations,* ed. Robert Forster and Orest Ranum (Baltimore, Md.: Johns Hopkins University Press, 1976), p. 141; see also Louise A. Tilly, "Individual Lives and Family Strategies in the French Proletariat," *Journal of Family History* 4 (Summer, 1979): 138.

control of labor power. Class associations and collective action were resources that offered Roubaix working-class families a way to combat
their individual vulnerability in the industrial capitalist economy.

Industrial Roubaix

Located in the northeastern department of the Nord, Roubaix was fab-
ulously successful in economic growth in the nineteenth century. In
the first third of the century, cotton spinning was the engine of Roubaix
industrialization. In the second third of the century, when British
competition became more threatening, Roubaix capitalists returned to
wool spinning and weaving. In this period, weaving was largely a domestic industry, done by hand in weavers' homes. Thus the Roubaix
region was studded with household "manufacturing" units. From the
1870s on, firms mechanized wool-weaving operations, and those employing rural hand loom weavers either disappeared or adopted the
new factory system. Wool dyeing and finishing firms developed. Finally, after 1872, the mechanization of wool combing was perfected. By
the end of the century, Roubaix was the principal wool city of France,
but an important, large-scale cotton industry also had been reintroduced and had prospered.[6]

An economic historian notes that Roubaix was characterized by
large firms of international importance, of which the best known were
"the establishments of Alfred Motte and Company (founded in 1879);
thirty-five years later, in France alone, they employed almost seven
thousand workers, of whom 70 percent were located in Roubaix and its
immediate environs. A mechanized wool combing mill (1800 workers),
a wool spinning mill, two cotton spinning mills, one knitting mill, two
cotton weaving shops, two very large dyeing factories (close to 1000
workers) represented the firm's industrial empire in Roubaix itself. . . .

[6]Jean Lambert-Dansette and Joseph-Antoine Roy, "Origines et évolution d'une
bourgeoisie: Le patronat textile du Bassin lillois (1789–1914)," *Revue du Nord* 37 (1955):
205–207, 210–11; J. A. Roy and J. Lambert-Dansette, "Origines et évolution d'une
bourgeoisie: Le patronat textile du Bassin lillois (1789–1914). III. La laine: Roubaix-
Tourcoing," *Revue du Nord* 40 (1958): 22–26. See also Felix-Paul Codaccioni, "Naissance
d'un triangle urbain (1815–1851)" and "Développement d'une nébuleuse urbaine
(1851–1914)," in *Histoire d'une métropole: Lille-Roubaix-Tourcoing*, ed. Louis Trenard
(Toulouse: Privat, 1977), pp. 317–46, 347–402.

The all powerful [Motte] family practically dominated the economy of the city."[7] Besides the extensive Motte empire and other large firms, however, there were also dozens of smaller units: "The factory created the city: one could count 27 weaving mills on the rue de la Fosse-aux-Chênes, 19 on the rue du Pays, etc."[8]

By 1900, the industry was not only mechanized but highly concentrated. The number of wool-spinning mills declined from forty-six to twenty-four between 1872 and 1900; but the number of workers almost doubled, and the number of spindles increased by 60 percent. In wool weaving, the number of mills fell in the same period from 229 to 102, with no decrease in workers or looms. The number of wool-combing mills increased by 28 percent, but the number of mechanical combs had come up by 95 percent.[9] The population of Roubaix boomed: it increased by 64 percent from 1872 to 1901 and by 1,380 percent over the century.

Despite Roubaix's rapid demographic growth and prosperity, modern economic historians have noted that it was characterized around 1900 by an "immobility of attitudes," lack of specialization, personal business organization rather than corporate, and too many small enterprises.[10] The nineteenth-century history of the city is a success story. Its epithet, the "American city," suggests just how unlike other French cities it seemed to contemporary observers.[11] Although it was exceptional in France because of the energy and success of its capitalists, its rapid industrialization and concentration, and its population growth,

---

[7]Codaccioni, "Une nébuleuse urbaine," p. 351. This quote and others that follow from French works are translated by the author.

[8]Ibid., p. 361. A similar comment is offered by Georges Franchomme in "L'évolution démographique et économique de Roubaix dans le dernier tiers du XIXe siècle," *Revue du Nord* 51 (1969): 232. He observes that in 1880 there were thirty weaving mills on the rue de la Fosse-aux-Chênes; seventeen on the rue du Pay; eleven on the rue des Lignes; eleven, rue de l'Hospice; nine, rue Nain; and nine, rue du Grand Chemin.

[9]Franchomme, "Roubaix," p. 240.

[10]Alain Hennebique, "A propos de la conjoncture économique dans l'arrondissement de Lille au début du XXe siècle," *Revue du Nord* 50 (1968): 75–87, and Franchomme, "Roubaix," pp. 237–39.

[11]Franchomme, "Roubaix," pp. 246–47. David Landes, "Religion and Enterprise: The Case of the French Textile Industry," in *Enterprise and Entrepreneurs in Nineteenth- and Twentieth-Century France*, ed. Edward C. Carter II, Robert Forster, and Joseph N. Moody (Baltimore, Md.: Johns Hopkins University Press, 1976), pp. 41–86, also emphasizes the originality of Roubaix.

Roubaix followed a trajectory common in the history of industrial capitalism. It is in that regard, as an industrial capitalist textile city, not as a typical French city, that Roubaix is the setting for this case study.

In addition to recent scholarly studies, Roubaix's population census, and police and administrative archives from the nineteenth century, several exceptionally rich sources offer approaches to the city's history. The writings of the Mottes, one of its self-conscious and self-assured business families, who themselves wrote in praise of their family virtues and business methods, provide personal and familial insight. The unpublished memoir of a working-class woman who has written her family history offers a view from the urban slum. Finally, a monograph written in the first decade of the twentieth century by one of the followers of the pioneering sociologist Frederic Le Play compares workers and industrialists.[12]

Le Play, in his conservative regret about what he perceived as the decline of the French patriarchal family since the Revolution of 1789, developed the monographic case method of sociological inquiry about families. He, his colleagues in this school of inquiry, and his successors wrote detailed case studies of individual families that included biographical accounts of the life of their adult members and reports on the current occupations, work, budget, and belongings of the household. Most of these studies focused on one family, usually peasants or artisans. Sometimes a monograph compared several families in one setting.

Paul Descamps, writing in 1909 and 1910 in the school's journal, *La science sociale*, hailed the monographic method for its *analytic* observation of facts. He noted that the journal had been criticized for focusing too strictly on simple types from which critics had deduced the belief that complex societies were beyond the school's capability to

---

[12] Fernand Motte, *Souvenirs personnels d'un demi-siècle de vie et de pensée, 1886–1942* (Lille: Silic, n.d. [1943]); Gaston Motte, *Les Motte: Etude de la descendance Motte-Clarisse, 1750–1950* (n.p., n.d.); Gaston Motte, *Motte-Bossut: Un homme, une famille, une firme* (Tourcoing: n.p., 1944); Jacques Toulemonde, *Naissance d'une métropole: Histoire économique et sociale de Roubaix et Tourcoing au XIXe siècle* (Tourcoing: Georges Frère, 1966); Madame G. [name disguised by an initial] (Unpublished manuscript, Roubaix, 1962); Madame G., personal interview, Roubaix, May, 1979; Paul Descamps, "La Flandre française: L'ouvrier de l'industrie textile," *La science sociale*, 24e Année, fasc. 59 (1909): 1–96; Paul Descamps, "La Flandre française: Les patrons de l'industrie textile," *La science sociale*, 25e Année, fasc. 66 (1910): 18–104.

observe and analyze. The school now was ready to go beyond its earlier work, he announced, though that early work was well justified by the logic of the simple before the complex. His monograph would answer the central question of contemporary industrial society: What have been the consequences of mechanization for human groups? As the geographic setting for his answer to this question, Descamps chose the arrondissement of Lille, the capital of the old province of French Flanders—in short, the location of Roubaix. This small area, he noted, contained 20 percent of all the steam horsepower in France.[13] Descamps, dealing as he was with a class society, insisted on the necessity of class comparisons. The chief rubric for the classifications of the Le Play school were those of inheritance systems, yet the study of workers alone revealed nothing about inheritance practices, for they had only their household goods to divide among their heirs. Thus one had to study the upper class, the holders of capital and landed property, to provide a complete picture of the situation of industrial Flanders. Further, he argued, employers play for workers something of the role that "place" (ecology) plays for agricultural peoples. For urban, industrial workers, the "*patronat* [employers] assumes the first place among active social factors."[14] Descamps's ethnographic gold mine is a detailed account of, on the one hand, the textile industry, its organization, and the capital and personal qualities required for setting up business, and on the other hand, the characteristics of work and workers. For both bosses and workers, personal and family life are placed in their material and organizational context.

The Rich

Our first overview of the entrepreneurial class of Roubaix is based on Descamps's writings. Following the logic of the Le Play model, a good deal of his effort goes into classifying employers, from simple to complex (i.e., from hand weavers who owned a loom to owners of great factories). The "modern" businessmen are defined as those with large, motor-driven factories. The size of the factory varied by the fiber and the process. Thus, the largest mills did wool combing (1,500 horse-

[13] Descamps, "L'ouvrier," pp. 3–4.
[14] Descamps, "Les patrons," pp. 18–19.

power, an investment of 4,000,000 francs, 900 workers). In declining order follow (1) cotton-spinning mills (600 horsepower, 1,500,000 francs' investment, 200 workers, 28,000 spindles); (2) wool-spinning mills (450 horsepower, 1,000,000 francs' investment, 150 workers, 17,000 spindles); (3) wool-weaving mills (260 horsepower, 300,000 francs' investment, 250 workers, 200 looms).[15] The way in which capital was concentrated in the northern textile industry, Descamps believed, presupposed not only a spirit of saving and a willingness to invest, but also personal virtue—"the development of administrative capability and a sense of responsibility." He echoed the local manufacturers' dictum that "to become the owner of a spinning mill, two things are necessary—a million [francs] and a bit of good sense," but added "plus character!" Judgmental and moralistic as this opinion seems, it certainly fits the Motte family's evaluation of its own success. It also fits recent scholarly assessments, which insist on the entrepreneurs' "profound originality."[16]

Let us follow Descamps's analysis of the entrepreneurial family, comparing it with testimony from the Motte family. Work, according to Descamps, was the essence of the life of the capitalist. The "intensity of industrial work . . . is unfavorable to the development of a philosophical spirit," he declared.[17] Eugène Motte, who served many years as mayor of Roubaix, wrote that the secret of the success of his father, Alfred, lay in "his faith in Roubaix, a city unique for work, a reservoir of unexhaustable labor . . . a city unique in the sense that the whole population breathes only to work, where no one avoids work through a government career or living off investments, where those who don't take up productive work are shunned . . . where one leaves no other inheritance to one's children than factories, primary materials, products and customers' orders."[18] Descamps concludes that, although vacations were more common in the twentieth century than they had been in the nineteenth century, most of the businessmen traveled little. Their homes were near their factories; they were at work at the same hour as their workers.

Although the wives of the textile entrepreneurs had created a

<hr>

[15] Ibid., p. 41.
[16] Ibid., pp. 43, 53. See Landes, "Religion and Enterprise," p. 51.
[17] Descamps, "Les patrons," p. 75.
[18] Gaston Motte, *Motte-Bossut*, p. 37.

worldly society, it was "not without certain particularities which strike outsiders."[19] That social world was firmly based on family connections. Descamps notes that these families had as many, or more, children as their workers, so there was little need to extend social life beyond kin. This is one of the major themes of descriptions of the business world of the Nord: family and kin are central organizing principles. Economic historian David Landes, for example, writes:

> The textile manufacturers of Roubaix-Tourcoing were, with rare exceptions, family entrepreneurs. The firm was an extension of the household, an extension that was usually juridically separate but that was identified so closely with it socially and operationally that it was sometimes hard to say where the one ended and the other began. . . .
>
> With the growth of large factories and the entry of children and grandchildren into firms that began as one-man, or more often, man-and-wife, enterprises, the physical separation of plant and household became marked. . . . The social identification . . . remained: the firm was at once the material support of the family and the basis of its status; the reputation, honor and strength of the one were the reputation, honor and strength of the other.[20]

Family and firm existed for each other.

The Mottes provide Landes with most of his illustrations, a limitation that, he argues, does not distort the picture, for they were a model for others. They intermarried with most of Roubaix's textile magnate families, as a glance at their genealogy shows: Cottigny, Danel, Dazin, Delfosse, Desurmont, Dewavrin, Duvillier, Flipo, Lemaire, Lepoutre, Lorthois, Masure, Pollet, Prouvost, Tiberghien, Toulemonde, Truche, Wattine, and Wibaux married Mottes.

In brief outline, this is the story of the Mottes, the well-documented prototype of the northern entrepreneurial family. It starts with cotton spinner Jean-Baptiste Motte-Brédart (1794–1864)—the wife's name was added to the male patronymic in each generation. His wife, Pauline Brédart, was the true entrepreneur, building the business for their eldest son, Louis Motte-Bossut, or Motte, as he was called as the senior son.

When his mill was destroyed by fire in 1845, Motte paid his creditors with the insurance and built the *filature monstre* ("the mon-

---

[19] Descamps, "Les patrons," p. 76.
[20] Landes, "Religion and Enterprise," pp. 50–51.

ster spinning mill"). He also built in time a weaving mill and a wool-spinning mill. Descamps comments on the pattern: "The wool textile magnates [of Roubaix] followed a continually successful trajectory which produced distinctive repercussions on the education and succession of their heirs. *The end they followed was to found as many mills as they had sons.*"[21] The four sons of Motte were "an inseparable team," according to their nephew, Gaston Motte. Each had his own industrial niche. Each also had his own civic role: Léon at the Tribunal de Commerce, Louis in Catholic charity, Georges in the chamber of commerce, and Edouard in city government. Gaston's Cousin Eugène was mayor of Roubaix. Edouard was also active in the association of owners of wool-spinning mills.[22]

Not all the Mottes were so successful, however. The second son of Motte-Brédart, Etienne, overextended himself in wool and failed in 1870. Alfred, the third son, first attempted to build vertically integrated mills, performing several processes, but he also failed. Both Etienne and Alfred were helped to make a new start by kin. Alfred developed his distinctive "system" of helping mechanically or entrepreneurially inclined men without capital to set up subsidiary mills with his financial backing. This proved successful and was combined with other businesses that sons, cousins, and nephews headed. The system, Descamps concludes, was especially well adapted to the milieu of Roubaix, for it built on family sentiment yet "had the flexibility necessary for modern industry."[23] Its ability to adapt was tested in the first years of the twentieth century when three of Motte's sons died, and the youngest son successfully reorganized and rationalized the firm, but still in family terms.[24] The family commitment to the textile business can be measured by the fact that of the heads of the eighty-one households that Gaston Motte reconstructed in his genealogy of four generations directly descended from the Motte-Clarisse marriage of 1784, 81.5 percent were men in textiles.[25]

The Mottes and the other Roubaix business clans were renowned

[21] Descamps, "Les patrons," p. 80. The family history outlined in the text is based on the Motte family writings, cited in footnote 12. In "Les patrons," Descamps also tells the Motte family history on pp. 82–85.

[22] Gaston Motte, *Motte-Bossut*, p. 106.

[23] Descamps, "Les patrons," p. 85.

[24] Landes, "Religion and Enterprise," pp. 65–66.

[25] Gaston Motte, *Les Motte*, p. 138.

for their large families. The social register listed families in order of size, "beginning with one or two with twenty-three or twenty-four children, another perhaps with twenty-one, several with nineteen or twenty, and going on to a dozen with fifteen or sixteen, a score with twelve and thirteen, and columns of names with seven, eight, nine or ten."[26] Gaston Motte calculated a more modest average of six children for the eighty-one Motte households he reconstructed that had lived over a 200–year period; there were only eleven with over ten children, including just one with fourteen.[27] A recent study finds that average births per wife in a sample of Nord bourgeois families actually *increased* over the century to a high point of 7.3 births for wives born 1869–78; child mortality reduced average completed family size even in this cohort to 6.6.[28] Bonnie Smith's richly documented monograph on women in these families shows how salient maternity was in their lives. She writes that the mother "held center stage in the family . . . [one] man complained that Northern society reeked of matriarchy in which women decided all questions of marriage and vocation, parental largesse, and parental love. . . . She was entrusted with . . . life in the most literal sense . . . [she] held the cord of life, or at least she stood as its most visible representative."[29]

Children were raised with family and firm before them as twin goals. As businesses prospered and grew in the nineteenth century, sons were sent first to Catholic boarding school and then, at about fifteen, to the mill. Although Alfred Motte (Motte's youngest brother), born in 1827, took a law degree in Paris, he was an exception. His early failures were in fact attributed to the fact that he did not go directly into the shop like his elder brothers.[30] Fernand Motte, Alfred's grand-

---

[26] Landes, "Religion and Enterprise," p. 43. See also Gaston Motte's calculations on the number of descendants of the Motte-Clarisse marriage in *Les Motte*, p. 139. Similar calculations of astronomic progressions were a popular genre of early twentieth-century populationist propaganda in its effort to combat the perceived demographic crisis in France. See Etienne Lamy, "La famille," in *La vie catholique dans la France contemporaine* (Paris: Bloud and Gay, 1918), pp. 138–40. Lamy remarks, "The custom of the industrialists is also that of the engineers, notaries and bankers" (p. 139).

[27] Gaston Motte, *Les Motte*, p. 137.

[28] Bonnie G. Smith, *Ladies of the Leisure Class: The Bourgeoises of Northern France in the Nineteenth Century* (Princeton, N.J.: Princeton University Press, 1981), p. 225.

[29] Ibid., pp. 63–64.

[30] Descamps, "Les patrons," p. 83.

son, born in 1886, went to a progressive Catholic school, but his father did not permit him to go beyond the baccalaureate. He finished at sixteen and a half and was sent to an internship in English factories, where he studied practical matters—techniques of weaving and dyeing.[31]

Education for girls was limited, but in quite a different way. Most attended Catholic boarding schools with long academic days and strict social rules. Subjects ranged from fancy needlework, sewing for the poor, and bookkeeping to literature, history, geography, languages, and some science. But, a critic writes, "instead of developing the mind, the convent aimed at polishing the surface and enhancing the external image of women. . . . Religious boarding schools correctly saw the difference between their system and the new trends in rational education for men."[32] When, in the early twentieth century, laic laws forced the end of convent education in France, the girls were sent to convents in nearby Belgium.[33]

Marriage was also a family-arranged affair. A glance at the Motte genealogy reveals frequently repeated patronymics, notations after a wife ("his first cousin"), and other indications of what Richard Cobb calls "the carefully limited horizons of the Roubaix-Tourcoing marriage network."[34] Children expected their parents, in consultation with kin (often an uncle who was a priest), to prescribe their marriage partners. Some, like Louise Dazin (1844–1917), whose physical development was believed too frail to sustain childbearing, were not permitted to marry.[35]

Marriage was an economic partnership, according to Smith: "People throughout the Nord ridiculed, in fact inveighed against, marriages occasioned by love." The women novelists of the Nord showed in fiction what misfortune could arise from lack of obedience to family interest. Everyone knew real cases of misalliance in love matches. There were few who questioned custom; after all, "What could better assure a successful union . . . than the careful selection of partners by parents who shared financial, political and social connections?" Young women

---

[31] Fernand Motte, *Souvenirs*, p. 24.

[32] Smith, *Ladies of the Leisure Class*, pp. 170, 171.

[33] Richard Cobb, "The Discreet Charm of the Bourgeoise," *New York Review of Books*, December 17, 1981, p. 57.

[34] Ibid.

[35] Gaston Motte, *Les Motte*, p. 74. See also Toulemonde, *Naissance d'une métropole*, pp. 181–83.

married young, at an average age of twenty-one, and in strict birth order, both indicators of parental control.[36]

The Motte family shared certain values—Gaston Motte enumer-
ates civic duty, family, Christian faith—but it also shared sociability,
mutual respect, and love. The statements of the oldest grandchildren
of Motte's household in the nineteenth century are evocative. His
table was "always open"; but one didn't talk about business in his
home. He believed "that the time devoted to his family was, in his life
of work, so parsimoniously measured that it would be wrong to rob it of
even a few moments spent in shop talk."[37] During each summer his
sons and their families made weekly visits to his country estate in Lannoy, and during the winter they went each Sunday to his Roubaix
home. The grandsons went by horse-drawn street car, challenging each
other to jump on and off while the car was in motion. The girls went,
more sedately, by carriage. The whole clan of cousins played together
in the woods of the estate. After the grandparents died, the four sons
and their families took turns staying in Lannoy through the spring and
summer. The children of the three sons, who died between 1901 and
1904, went to their childless aunt, Marie Pollet-Motte, for advice
and support. (At her death at age 85 in 1940, Madame Pollet-Motte
had 1,388 nieces, nephews, nephews- and nieces-in-law, grandnieces
and grandnephews, and once, twice, and thrice removed nieces and
nephews, 448 of them Mottes!) It was clearly advantageous to be a
Motte; familial and financial rewards abounded. The family strategies,
social and business, and the kin network were instruments to validate
and exalt their way of life. Both sociability and business moved along
kin lines. Thus, Gaston Motte concludes with satisfaction, was the patriarchal atmosphere created by his grandfather carried on.[38]

The story of the younger branch of Mottes, descended from Motte's
youngest brother Alfred, is similar. Fernand Motte recalls dinners
at the homes of the patriarch, Alfred, at which children and adults
gathered at the groaning board. Plenteous food was one of the few
Motte extravagances, at least in the nineteenth century. Fernand's father was rather stingy (an eccentricity noted elsewhere in the family
by another cousin, Jacques Toulemonde), so much so that his family

[36] Smith, *Ladies of the Leisure Class*, pp. 58–60.
[37] Gaston Motte, *Motte-Bossut*, p. 143.
[38] Ibid., p. 147.

spent vacations with cousins who shared the rent on cottages at the beach. Fernand notes that "sharing property was current practice then," but he adds that later the purse strings were loosened and a more extravagant life-style became the norm. His sister's marriage, for example, was the occasion for completely renovating and redecorating the family's Roubaix home.[39] A family member summed up, in 1914, the essence of the Mottes this way: "They were always united among themselves; they knew how to defend their ideas. . . . Older and younger sons were cautious in business, always following the latest technical developments, seeking to open new markets . . . once they made a decision, they acted with a certain audacity, energy and perseverance. . . . This devotion to their business and its constant expansion in no way prevented them from caring for their own hearth, —shaping the education of their children, taking part in family gatherings, being devoted to each other and gay in society."[40]

The Mottes certainly worked together with amazing success to socialize their children to family values and to promote the family interest in business and marriage. Their family economy was a high-powered, smoothly running engine; their strategies were elevated in the lifetime of the third generation into Roubaix and French myth. Whether or not the myth is entirely to be believed (there are a few discordances in the account), the Mottes used their economic resources and personal qualities strategically to establish a political presence and to aggrandize their wealth. In the process, family and kin were one more resource.

The Workers

Descamps's account of worker families in French Flanders follows the same logic as his study of their bosses. It starts with a meticulous description of the organization of work in the textile industry, with careful specification of the qualifications needed by workers. Skill, attentiveness, ability to command, and strength are the qualities that he believed determined who could do a task properly; each varied systematically by age and sex to produce a neatly segregated labor force.

[39] Fernand Motte, *Souvenirs*, pp. 13, 19.
[40] Clément Dazin, quoted in Gaston Motte, *Les Motte*, p. 141.

Descamps observed the cotton-spinning process in the huge mill of Wibaux-Florin, a relative of the Mottes. In the preparation of the rough thread, mechanization was very advanced; no apprenticeship was needed for the first process, pulling the cotton out of bats and twisting it into ribbons, then rough threads, as it moved from one machine to another. The main task for workers was tying the threads that broke; the spindle stopped spinning when that happened so sustained attention was not necessary. The bobbins were then transferred to the spinning room proper where there were two types of machines. The workers' chief task there also was tying broken threads, but more attention was required to notice when this was necessary because the spindle did not halt automatically with a broken thread. Teams of five workers were assigned to each "self-acting" spinning machine: one spinner, two piecers, and two bobbin girls or boys. At ages thirteen to sixteen, children worked at replacing the filled bobbins; if boys were quick and attentive, they were promoted to piecing. At twenty-five to thirty, men moved on to become spinners, "in command" of the team and responsible for its output. Technically, no apprenticeship was needed for spinning, but the "gift of organization and command" was necessary. It was possible, Descamps wrote, for women to have such a gift, but the selection and promotion process from bobbin worker to piecer to spinner left women at the lowest level. Employers believed that women worked for relatively short periods except when they were young; thus, they kept women circulating in the lower ranks rather than moving up.[41] Actually, women were doing wage work in a discontinuous way over much of their lives, but employers acted as though they were temporary, thus perpetuating girls' and women's circulation at the base of the job hierarchy.

Similar detailed description of wool carding, combing, and weaving processes was based on direct observation of Roubaix mills. The wool industry employed some workers who were more skilled, such as the *trieur* (wool sorter) who was trained in an apprenticeship of two to four years. The *trieur*'s task was to align wool fibers of different lengths into uniform ribbons of wool. Women were technically capable of the work, but, again, employers refused to train them because they expected

[41] Descamps, "L'ouvrier," pp. 9–11.

them to quit after several years in the mill.[42] Other workers in the combing mill, many of them women, were simply machine minders. Contemporaries believed that jobs in the woolen mills were more desirable and respectable for women and girls than those in the cotton mills. The women's task required so little attention that the machines were allowed to run through meal breaks without minders.[43] The final spinning of wool was a more delicate process than that of cotton, and the thread broke more easily. The spinning team included one spinner, four piecers, and two bobbin boys or girls. Some women became piecers, unlike employment in cotton mills, but advancement to spinner was more highly selective for wool (the ratio of spinners to piecers was one to four) and no women became spinners.

From the spinning mill, the woolen thread was sent to the weaving mill, or *fabrique*, as it was known in Roubaix. The mill Descamps visited employed thirteen hundred workers: five hundred male weavers and four hundred men and four hundred women concerned with loom preparation and accessory tasks. The warp was prepared by men; the woof was measured by men and wound by hand onto shuttles by women. The wool weaver was a skilled worker who had to pay close attention to the quality of cloth being produced and adjust the loom to correct and prevent mistakes. He had to mend broken thread while the machine moved. Boys learned to weave under supervision on small looms until about age sixteen, when they were left on their own. There was only one skilled female occupation, the *piqûreuse* or *piqûrière* who did hand repair or mending of faults in the cloth. It required a serious apprenticeship, but, Descamps writes, inasmuch as it was essentially fine sewing, married women could continue to do the task at home once they were trained. Therefore, employers were willing to train women in the skill.[44]

Thus all the textile industry employed a labor force hierarchically organized by age and sex. Children and the young of both sexes formed the base; in cotton mills, only young men moved on to be piecers and later spinners. In wool mills, young women became piecers, but they were denied spinner status. Only men were weavers. The aristocrats of female labor, the *piqûrières*, were more accurately termed seam-

---

[42] Ibid., p. 13.
[43] Ibid., pp. 16–17.
[44] Ibid., p. 17.

stresses than textile workers, and many of them worked outside the factory.

These conditions of work mesh neatly with the actual patterns of employment by age, sex, and marital status in Roubaix worker households, according to the 1906 population census. Adult males were universally wage earners, unless they were ill or handicapped. In households with children, there was a cyclical pattern in which mothers and children alternated as wage earners. If there were only one or two children and family consumption needs were large, wives continued to work. As the children became teenagers and entered the mills, most wives discontinued steady work; they were seldom regular wage earners in working-class families. Wives worked when need was great, stopped when they could. Except for minders, women's earning prospects in textile work leveled off sharply after adolescence. Their household responsibilities did not decrease as their children became workers, because those children tended to live at home. Textile family strategies allocated wage labor outside the home to adult males and adolescent and young adult children, rather than to wives. Wives provided household services for employed members of their family, a division of labor that made sense considering women's lack of opportunity for remunerative wage labor. These mothers had children living in their household most of their married life.

Although children were wage earners who contributed to the family welfare, from performing an adult's day of labor they acquired little autonomy or freedom of action. They were expected to live at home, and indeed 92 percent of males and 83 percent of females aged fifteen to nineteen lived with their parents. (The percentage for both sexes in age from ten to fourteen was 97 percent.) Only 1 percent of young men and 3 percent of young women (aged fifteen to nineteen) lived in their own households, and in the case of the women, all were married. The difference in proportions of men and women living with parents lies mostly with the 8 percent of women, many of them Belgian, who were domestic servants.[45] The servant from the Belgian countryside, saving

[45] This section and others referring to the 1906 census are based on computer analysis of a 10 percent sample of households from the nominal list of the 1906 census for Roubaix. A fuller discussion of findings from this analysis can be found in Louise A. Tilly, "The Family Wage Economy of a French Textile City, Roubaix, 1872–1906," *Journal of Family History* 4 (Winter, 1979): 381–94; idem, "Individual Lives and Family Strategies

her wages as a nest egg to attract a good husband, was a regular member of upper bourgeois households. The nephew of Louise Dazin wrote that she, a single woman, had three female servants, one of whom terrorized her young visitors, boys and girls.[46] Working-class children, then, were expected to live at home while they worked and contribute all or most of their wages to the family budget. Only migrant young women were able to accumulate savings—at the price of being domestic servants. Economically motivated parental control over children as workers continued up to the age of marriage. Once they married, however, children set up new households separate from their parents.

The conjugal family appears to have been the main source of mutual support and assistance in the working class. Families could claim their children's wages when they lived at home; the age patterns of children's coresidence with their parents also suggest that parents tried to prevent, and usually succeeded in preventing, their children's marriage at a young age. This could lead to disputes between the generations, as Madame G., a Roubaix working-class woman born in 1922, has testified. In 1979 I spoke with her and read the family history she had written sixteen years earlier. She wished to remain anonymous. Her family was hardworking and stable, and some of their misfortunes were due to the Depression. Nevertheless, the way of life she describes for the 1920s and 1930s echoes in a poignant way Descamps's earlier account.

She notes that her parents' young age at marriage (in 1920, they were twenty and twenty-two) was at least partly due to alienation from their parents. Her mother, Madame G. notes, was estranged at least temporarily from her own widowed mother when she insisted on marrying at twenty.[47] Madame G. herself went out to work at age thirteen, as soon as she was legally permitted. Control of children's choices and dependence on their wages were features of industrial Roubaix well

in the French Proletariat," pp. 137–52; Tamara K. Hareven and Louise A. Tilly, "Solitary Women and Family Mediation in American and French Textile Cities," *Annales de Démographie Historique* (1981): 253–71; and Louise A. Tilly, "Women, Family Strategies and Industrialization in France: Schoolteachers and Shopkeepers, 1906" (Paper delivered at the Eighth International Congress of Economic History, Budapest, August 16–20, 1982).

[46] Toulemonde, *Naissance d'une métropole*, pp. 180–81.

[47] Madame G., manuscript, p. 2.

into the twentieth century. In contrast to the wealthy families of Roubaix, worker families were relatively unconcerned about their children's choice of a marriage partner. They worried about their children leaving the family economy rather than about appropriate marriages. This is not to suggest that workers married for love while the rich married for economic partnership. The worker marriage was also an economic partnership, with a customary division of labor—a male wage earner and a female serving and saving—but the young workers were freer to choose than were the young bourgeois.

Choice of spouse was one of the few choices a worker could make. Madame G. describes her youth as deprived of opportunity of choice. She contracted tuberculosis in the crowded, unsanitary, and poorly heated slum in which her family lived. The special school to which she was sent, a "fresh air" school, neglected academic learning. Other Roubaix families may have been better able to facilitate opportunity for their sons at least by assuring them schooling. Descamps notes that formal technical schooling made young men eligible for much better jobs: "Certificates and diplomas are the key."[48] To earn such certification, however, boys had to stay in school until age sixteen or seventeen, a circumstance rarely achieved in working-class families because of their need for children's wages. Some families in which the husband was a worker mangaged to set up the wives as small shopkeepers or cabaret keepers. This arrangement could provide the extra margin of income to keep a son in school. Indeed, the 1906 census showed a pronounced pattern of households in which wives of workers were independent shopkeepers, possibly illustrative of such a family strategy designed to advance sons. It is also possible, of course, that wives chose this form of earning money for other family needs because it was less disruptive to their ability to carry out housework and child care duties.

Child-woman ratios and aggregate birthrates for 1906 suggest that working-class women were already controlling their fertility quite substantially compared with the women of earlier periods. The household size revealed by the census was modest compared with the wealthy bourgeois household. Madame G. describes a good deal of physical deprivation, ill health, and economic uncertainty as characteristic of

[48] Descamps, "L'ouvrier," p. 46.

stable working-class family life in Roubaix. Her parents started married life with very few belongings, and their acquisition of furnishings and comforts was painfully slow because two children were born in quick succession. Children were clearly burdens for many years as they grew up. The family succeeded in saving to buy household needs by dint of the mother's sending the two small daughters to foster care in the country and going out to work herself. Only later did the family have a third child. They lived in a *courée*, the distinctive row housing of Roubaix, which was built back-to-back into blocks perpendicular to the street front. The tiny individual units made it possible to crowd hundreds of people into a very small area.[49] Madame G. shares with Descamps the view that the housing was the cause of not only poor health but of demoralization. He writes in praise of the worker family that can leave the worker *courée* to live in an independent "*home* [English word used in the French text]; the children, released from the promiscuity of the common court, experience family education, rather than that of the street."[50] The availability of better housing was a turning point for Madame G.'s family, a moment they greeted with relief and joy. Their efforts at mobility were focused quite simply on improving their material living conditions.

The working-class family was likely to be less religious than the bourgeois family. Madame G. writes that her parents did not believe in God (and certainly a large proportion of Roubaix working *men*, at least, did not practice Catholicism), but they had their values: "courage, cleanliness, honor, duty." Nevertheless, the picture she paints is one of people greatly constrained by circumstances and without much hope. She writes of the "inferiority complex" of the proletariat, of those who had nothing. As a girl, Madame G. resented the handouts of clothing her mother accepted from the wealthy. She also pitied her parents for their passivity before poverty and the constant necessity to work that made them, she writes with passion, like "automatons."[51]

Compared with the wealthy, Roubaix worker families faced the world disarmed by their economic vulnerability. They were not without resources; nor were they simply always reacting. Their chief re-

[49] Jacques Prouvost, "Les courées à Roubaix," *Revue du Nord* 51 (1969): 307–16.
[50] Descamps, "L'ouvrier," p. 61.
[51] Madame G., manuscript, p. 28.

source was their own conjugal family. The pattern of allocating roles between husband and wife in the family illustrates their strategic rationality and so do the demands they made on children and the pattern of tapping wives' labor as storekeepers.

Families and Class-based Collective Action

Although they were poor and unlikely to have large kin networks nearby, working-class families were not without resources. These families, or members of them, were also collective actors, in more positive assertions of their interests. The sources are silent on individuals, except for a few leaders in the cooperative movement, unions, and socialist party; it is to group patterns that we must turn. Collective activities probably seldom involved a majority of Roubaix worker families (with the possible exception of the election, by universal manhood suffrage, of a socialist mayor in 1894). Nevertheless, the range of activities and the ways in which class-based organizations and action touched private life suggest very broad involvement in them.

The textile union, the "syndicat ouvrier textile de Roubaix," was founded in 1872. Its headquarters were in the *estaminet* (a northern term for café) La Paix. The union reported 10,584 members in 1907, each of whom paid one-quarter franc per week dues, which primarily was used for a strike fund. It also provided assistance to workers and their families in case of hardship, sickness, injury, or military service of a son whose wages were then lost to his family. A fifteen-franc payment was also made to women at the birth of a child.[52] The testimony of the textile union before the 1904 Parliamentary Commission on the Textile Industry illustrates its family concerns. Wool weavers, the report states, were increasingly expected to tend two looms, an intensification of the rhythm of work and the effort needed to perform it. The union expressed its alarm that one of the consequences of this practice was the almost complete disappearance of apprenticeship and opportunities for child labor. The number of workers was also being reduced in the spinning process; again, the strength needed to operate the new machines meant that adult males were directly recruited and the old

[52] Descamps, "L'ouvrier," pp. 64–66.

system of working up to the spinner slot was no longer possible in newer installations. The loss was to the sons of workers.[53] Although they had no property to pass on to their sons then, textile workers vigorously opposed employer decisions and technical change that militated against opportunities to place their children.

The majority of strikes in the period did not directly touch family issues. Demands for better wages (or against cuts), or for continued control over the rhythm and pace of work, and protests against harassment by employers were more common. A closer look at some of the strikes suggests some of the interdependence of family and these apparent strictly work issues.

The October, 1903, Roubaix general strike protested the new pay scale imposed by the bosses. A good deal of the action in the strike was the strikers' effort to get other workers to join them. They shouted at workers as they entered the factory, broke windows of shops that were working, sacked offices, and dumped records. These efforts went also into residential neighborhoods, where nonstrikers were harassed by taunting serenades, recalling the charivari. Controllable labor power was a resource to strikers, just as it was in families. The family whose members struck—or who refused to strike—shared in the consequences of this decision, whether it was physical suffering from lost wages or harassment from militants who accused them of lack of solidarity.[54]

A long bitter strike ran from February 28 to September 25, 1907, at the Ternyck weaving mill. The issue was a new *tarif* (pay scale) through which the employers hoped to establish incentives for the "best" workers, as they defined them, and lower wages for less able workers, in particular old weavers and Belgians. The strikers insisted that standard hourly pay be continued. Everyone had his off days; everyone would get old. Equal wages were the best policy. They wished to establish and police standards themselves. A compromise was worked

[53] "Rapport de la Chambre syndicale ouvrière textile de Roubaix et Environs, à la Commission d'Enquête Parlementaire textile," n.d., from ADN [Archives départementales du Nord] M 625/1. The Commission visited Roubaix on January 20, 1904.

[54] The 1903 general strike in Roubaix is described in newspaper articles found in ADN M 625/18: *Le Progrès du Nord* (Lille), October 11, 1903, and *Supplement du Journal L'Egalité de Roubaix-Tourcoing* (Roubaix), October 16, 1903.

out, but worker control was diminished as a consequence. Workers'
vulnerability to wages that declined with age increased.[55]

Workers in the Lepoutre weaving mill protested their bosses' harassment. There the boss had devised a steam jet, irritating and potentially capable of burning, in the latrine to discourage what he believed
to be too frequent visits by workers on Mondays. (The argument went
that workers drank too much on Sunday and so urinated too much on
Monday!) The workers' list of complaints accused Lepoutre of tyranni-
cal policies. Factory discipline and efforts to control workers' home
lives were at issue. The company, they complained, was not only constantly looking over their shoulder at work, but it also had a full-scale
spy system that inquired about workers' opinions, their families, and
their personal behavior outside of work. The strikers were a minority
of the 610 workers in the plant, but they tried by propaganda and occasionally by violence to persuade their co-workers to join them.[56]

Worker solidarity was by no means complete in Roubaix; activists
were often isolated. The issues they struck over were primarily about
working conditions, but family issues often lay behind them. Militants'
families were a resource; suffering families could also make one hesi-
tate to strike or make the end of a strike with no change in conditions
bitter.

The late nineteenth-century Guesdist socialists of Roubaix—followers of Jules Guesde, their parliamentary deputy—established many
cooperative institutions. After 1904, when a unified socialist "French
Section of the Workers' International" emerged, the older cooperative
ways continued. The "jewel" of Roubaix socialist cooperatives was La
Paix, which included the *estaminet*, the union headquarters, and a
bakery. The co-op did two million francs of business yearly, and thirty-
five hundred families were members.[57] Cooperatives were not a socialist monopoly. The first cooperative bakery had been established in

[55] ADN M 625/87. The Ternyck strike issues are described in a workers' committee
report dated May 16, 1907, and in later reports from police and newspapers.

[56] Lepoutre troubles and strike information in ADN M 625/92: a report from
L'Egalité de Roubaix-Tourcoing (Roubaix), August 7, 1910; an undated "Appeal to Workers"; a handwritten list of demands dated July 27, 1910, and addressed to the prefect of
the Nord; and police reports dated July 25, September 6, 9, and 22, and October 8,
1910.

[57] Descamps, "L'ouvrier," p. 76.

1865. L'Union, another cooperative bakery, was established in 1892 by the Syndicat Mixte of Roubaix (an employer-worker organization also known as the yellow union by the socialists). Their 1906 report claimed that they produced and sold more bread at cheaper prices than did La Paix. L'Union shareholders did not receive rebates, as did those of La Paix, for this profit was reserved to provide free bread to members in temporary need. L'Union was the largest cooperative in Roubaix, indeed in all of France; fifteen thousand families were members of L'Union.[58] The success of cooperatives, both those of the socialists and those of the bosses, shows family readiness to accept collective efforts at economy.

Food prices were an issue of great concern to working-class families, and it was this issue that provoked the largest class-based women's protest in the period before the First World War. In the late summer of 1911, the prices of meat and butter increased sharply in the Nord, partly as a consequence of an epidemic among cattle and consequent impounding of meat from diseased carcasses. A popular movement protesting the high prices began in the southern part of the department in metalworking cities. By September 1, socialists had taken the lead in Roubaix by calling a meeting, attended by two thousand housewives, at La Paix. A socialist report to the group illustrated graphically how prices had risen over the past months. The group set up a women's committee and resolved to hold a public demonstration the following Sunday. A delegation took the resolution to the city hall, requesting that it be forwarded to the departmental prefect in Lille and to the government in Paris. One woman was reported to have urged her listeners to bring their children to the demonstration; if there was no response to their demands they should be ready to strike out physically at the authorities.[59]

The women's demonstration, a week later, was followed by violent incidents in the evening. The demonstrators divided into small groups, making it difficult for police to follow and disperse them. One group attacked a butcher shop and broke down the door. The houses of

[58] For the origins of cooperatives in Roubaix, see Alfred Renouard and L. Moy, *Les institutions ouvrières et sociales du Département du Nord* (Lille: Danel, 1889), pp. 28–88. See also Paul Bou, "Un centre d'action sociale à Roubaix, la boulangerie cooperative, 'l'Union,'" *L'action populaire*, 126 (1906): 9–11, and Descamps, "L'ouvrier," p. 81.

[59] *La Lanterne* (Paris), September 9, 1911, from AN [Archives nationales] F^{12}7025.

certain butter merchants and butchers were stoned. A barricade was erected to fend off the authorities; demonstrators stoned police from behind it.[60] A formal agreement on retail prices was eventually negotiated by shopkeepers and the women's committee. Many shopkeepers, however, simply refused to sell certain items rather than conform to the fixed price. A circular distributed at factory gates urged housewives to demand that their shopkeepers honor the agreement. The Roubaix section of the socialist party passed a resolution disapproving violent acts by individuals as contrary to socialist policy. They nevertheless assailed police brutality and urged workers to continue energetically their action against price hikes. This should be done without violence, the socialist leaders urged, reminding their followers that the high price of food was not the fault of small shopkeepers, but of "rich bourgeois speculators, who alone were truly responsible for the current events."[61]

During the period before the war, socialists competed with the Roman Catholic Church and its capitalist allies to rally workers to their side; each used social and political institutions that offered aid and sociability to families. The socialists spoke to workers both at the factory and at the *estaminet*; their Sunday meetings were poorly attended at first, so they introduced entertainment such as dances or concerts at the end of the meetings, an effort "to satisfy all the members of the worker family."[62] Socialist morality plays that presented parables of the class struggle were warmly acclaimed, as were popular singers in *patois*. Roubaix's most famous *chanteur*, Louis Catrice, the son of a weaver, wove hard-edged *patois* into humorously sarcastic or hotly angry verse.[63] The socialists thus offered a popular sociability for families along with their propaganda.

They also organized neighborhood sections in which militants could teach socialist principles to their neighbors or work in election campaigns. A myriad of associated societies sprang up: drum and bugle corps, choruses, homing pigeon clubs, and more intellectual groups

[60] *La Lanterne* (Paris), September 9, 1911, and *Paris-Journal*, September 9, 1911, found in AN F^{12}7025.

[61] *La Lanterne* (Paris), September 17, 1911, from AN F^{12}7025.

[62] Nicole Quillien, "La S.F.I.O. à Roubaix de 1905 à 1914," *Revue du Nord* 51 (1969): 278. See also Gustave Siauve (Evausy), *Roubaix Socialiste* (Lille: n.p., 1896), for a discussion of socialists' efforts in the first socialist mayoralty term.

[63] Jean Piat, *Roubaix: Capitale du Textile* (Roubaix: La Mairie, 1968), pp. 60–61.

such as "free thought" clubs flourished. The socialists also sponsored youth groups and sports clubs, apparently with less success than similar efforts by Catholics, who managed to recruit children at much younger ages and keep their loyalty through adolescence.[64] Although or perhaps because she despaired at her parents' passivity, Madame G. became a militant. She was recruited to political action through the Catholic Worker Youth movement (Jeunesse ouvrière chrétienne) and later became a socialist. Under that party's banner, she was elected to the city council of the commune where she now lives, which is adjacent to Roubaix. For her, and for other activists in class-based organizations, collective action was a way to improve both work and family prospects.

Conclusion

Rich and poor in Roubaix sought to maintain and promote their economic and social interests. The wealthy carefully controlled their children's choices and socialized them to a pride of the clan. The extended kin and the values the family stood for became an all-enveloping structure that prescribed family loyalty and praised individual achievement. The working-class family also structured the lives of its members, but in a unique way: by using labor power as a resource. Workers also acted in the interest of the family. There were several paths for this action. It nearly always meant limiting children's choices about work and schooling and wives' choices between wage labor and home work. Children's and wives' behavior consistently responded to family needs. Action could involve strategies at the level of the conjugal family for mobility in the next generation. Finally, it could involve going beyond the conjugal family, not to kin as the wealthy did, but to networks of work place, community, and class to collective action. Hedged in by poverty, uncertainty, and decisions imposed on them by their employers, worker families nevertheless opened and maintained space in their way of life so their own strategies could give them some control.

[64] Quillien, "La S.F.I.O.," pp. 281–82.

Dating Becomes the Way
of American Youth

> *I never go with any girls,*
> *I never make a date.*
> *I'm never fussing on the squad*
> *Or saying "ain't love great?"*
> *I never take one to a dance,*
> *The reason's plain to see.*
> *I never go with girls because*
> *The girls won't go with me.*
> —from *Minneapolis Central High News*, 1923

DATING was already becoming prescriptive behavior for urban high school students when a Minneapolis boy published this comic lament in his high school newspaper in 1923.[1] His nonfeasance was to be explained neither by simple preference on his part, nor by any characteristic of the dating system itself: only a personal flaw could explain why one did not date. In high school, if one hoped to be favorably recognized by one's peers, one dated—and this, if anything, was even truer for girls than for boys. "I am . . . considered not bad looking or a bad dresser. But somehow I just can't be popular either with boys or girls. I would love to, but I simply can't. I don't know what is the matter. All my girl acquaintances always talk about their beaus and dates,

As I wrote this paper, my scope was widened, my notions challenged, and my nerve steeled by the advice and criticism of Saundra-Lynn Coulter, Ellen DuBois, Judith Modell, and Sabra Waldfogel. And, as always, the historian counts upon the assistance of many others in the effort to locate and come to terms with material. In this case, I owe a special debt to Faustino Alvarez of the Minnesota Historical Society; David J. Klaassen of the Social Welfare History Archives, University of Minnesota; and Philip M. Voxland of the Social Science Research Facilities Center, University of Minnesota.

[1]Tauno Pajari, "Who Doo," *Minneapolis Central High News*, January 25, 1923. I read about ten years each of six Minnesota high school newspapers, four from the Twin Cities and two from small cities outstate (in nonmetropolitan areas), all maintained at the Minnesota Historical Society.

but I don't have any. I'm always by myself."[2] My essay seeks to eluci-
date the terms of the dating system in its early years, to discuss the
reasons for and to describe the pattern of its spread, and to consider
some of its cultural and personal implications.

I

"The outside world of today has no use for flimsy worshipers of petty
idols such as 'popularity.'" thundered a Minneapolis Central High edi-
torialist in 1923, but popularity was the universally understood term
for what the great majority of high schoolers sought to a greater or
lesser degree. Such editorial fulmination was, of course, to no avail.
"Many individuals as soon as they attain 'popularity' turn down their
friends of former days and never even seem to recognize them again,"
the editorial claimed, but at the same time other high-school editorial-
ists were excoriating the tendency to cliquishness that evidently characterized their schools then as now.[3] Popularity and cliquishness were
closely related and tied closely to dating: both were parts of a new system of social relations governed informally but firmly by young people
themselves. Not all youth saw dating in the same light, to be sure,
even in the high schools. Material wherewithal made a difference, as
we shall see; so also did cultural heritage. And asymmetries of gender
roles were the armature around which the dating system evolved. But
for the moment let us simply note that well before the adult world took
much notice,[4] most boys and girls from their mid-teens on came to
organize their social lives around an institution not of their elders'
making, one that was to reorient—partially—the road to marriage.

The defining characteristic of the new dating system and, what is
more critical, of the graduated series of dates that might lead to a

---

[2] "All Alone" to Doris Blake, "Doris Blake's Love Answers," *New York Daily News*,
May 21, 1925.

[3] *Minneapolis Central High News*, December 20, 1923; *Little Falls The Comet's Tail*,
February 24, 1928; *St. Paul Central High Times*, April 4, 1925, and September 28,
1927; *Minneapolis Central High News*, December 15, 1925.

[4] Scholarly observation of dating began with the inquiry into 1930s' college dating
carried out by the sociologist Willard Waller. Although Waller described dating as a special case of dissipation, he nonetheless established the crucial point that it was peer-
supervised, rule-governed behavior. Waller, "The Rating and Dating Complex," *American Sociological Review* 2 (1937): 727–34; idem, *The Family* (New York: The Dryden

closer relationship between young men and women was that a date was away from home, unchaperoned, and not subject to parental veto; it depended upon the free election of the participants. Certainly, *some* American boys and girls of the middle classes had coupled in every imaginable way without parental awareness before the turn of the century, but "dates" of this sort lacked the continuity and regularity that the full evolution of the dating system would permit after World War I. Under the older system, there was no normatively sanctioned way to get "serious" about someone without doing so at least occasionally at home and with parental approval. Chaperonage asserted parents' oversight of what boys and girls might do together, and the home visit assured girls' parents of some control over whom their daughters might be seeing. Both were important, and both vanished with dating, which substituted peer oversight. Not the occurrence of emotional or physical intimacy but the question of whose advice guided young people in developing heterosexual ties was the critical difference between dating and "keeping company," which it supplanted.[5]

When 1920s' parents asserted chaperonage or oversight, they were repulsed. The young unmarried woman "considers the whole matter a farce," reported an earnest "young matron" to her discussion group in 1922. She continued, "There is little respect for the chaperone, whose presence has no effect whatever upon the actions of the young people. The chaperone is considered mainly as a sop to the older generation."[6] And efforts to bring the date into the home in the face of the spread of commercial amusement and the prosperity to get to it proved hopeless gestures: "A mother [cannot] . . . oppose her in the progress of this affair which the girl takes so seriously. But one thing she can do; she can have the man or the boy, if it is only a boy, constantly invited to the house. When the girl compares him with her father or brothers he may

Press, 1938), chap. 9; Michael Gordon, "Was Waller Ever Right? The Rating and Dating Complex Reconsidered," *Journal of Marriage and the Family* 43 (1981): 67–76; Samuel Harmon Lowrie, "Dating Theories and Student Responses," *American Sociological Review* 16 (1951): 334–340.

[5] Gordon in "Was Waller Ever Right?" is more concerned with intimacy than with the system governing it, and therefore finds dating-like relationships in the nineteenth century.

[6] Minutes of December 15, 1922, meeting, Chapter (Study Group) 13, Child Study Association of America, in Folder 282, Child Study Association Collection, Social Welfare History Archives, University of Minnesota.

fall short of the standards of taste or education which they maintain."[7] Parents shortly abandoned these checks as they surrendered the more direct aspects of their oversight of their adolescent children. A chapter in Emily Post's 1923 edition was titled "Chaperons and Other Conventions." By 1927, it was "The Vanishing Chaperon and Other New Conventions," and by 1937 "The Vanished Chaperon and Other Lost Conventions."[8] In 1932 a government advice pamphlet described the new pattern of youth behavior (including petting) as a "wholesome" abandonment of "Victorian" patterns, and a sensible aspect of mate selection. (The advice, to be sure, was somewhat in the van of public opinion on the petting issue.) The "crush," once the subject of utter condescension, had now to be seen as a valuable developmental episode, and dating as the occasion for mature choice.[9]

The date itself had a compelling logic quite distinct from that of prior forms: it was a step in an ongoing negotiation with rules defined and deviations punished by age peers. The logic of the date anchored it in pleasure and centered the choices it occasioned in the daters themselves (within limits imposed by the peer culture). The home visit or chaperoned dance, in essence, had been either purely sociable—part of a group occasion—or overtly related to courtship. The date might

---

[7] Caroline Benedict Burrell, *Our Girls and Our Times* (Boston: W. A. Wilde Co., 1927), pp. 63–64.

[8] Emily Post, *Etiquette* (New York: Funk & Wagnalls, 1923); idem, *Etiquette*, new and enlarged ed. (New York: Funk & Wagnalls, 1927); idem, *Etiquette* (New York: Funk & Wagnalls, 1937). The shifts between 1927 and 1937 are particularly revealing: "Ethically the only chaperon is the young girl's own sense of dignity and pride. The girl who has the right attitudes of character needs no chaperon—ever" (1927, p. 288). "From an ethical standpoint, the only chaperon worth having in this present day is a young girl's own efficiency in chaperoning herself. The girl who has been trained to appraise every person and situation she meets . . . needs no one to sit beside her and tell her what to do" (1937, p. 354). Post epitomized "the most important change in the whole chaperon situation" as "training is taking the place of protection" (p. 353), or the empowering of the adolescent girl within her own family or orientation.

[9] D. C. Thom, *Guiding the Adolescent* (Washington, D.C.: U.S. Department of Labor, Children's Bureau, Publication No. 225, 1933), pp. 84–85; Theodore L. Smith, "Types of Adolescent Affection," *Pedagogical Seminary* 11 (1904): 178–203; Marion Dowd, "Concerning the Socio-moral Life and Behavior of the Adolescent," *Education* 49 (1928): 65–78; Eleanor Rowland Wembridge, "Suggested Improvements in Jane Doe and Her Boy Friend," *Survey* 61 (1929): 719–21; Eugenie A. Leonard and Margaret Bond Brockway, "Must a Girl Pet To Be Popular?" *The Parents' Magazine* 71 (June, 1932): 20; Henry F. Pringle, "What Do the Women of America Think about Morals?" *Ladies Home Journal* 54 (May, 1938): 14–15.

turn out to be either of these, or both, or something else again, but what it turned out to be depended upon how well the negotiation at its core went, a negotiation regarding immediate pleasure. By definition, boys planned and paid for "a good time" and asked of their girls a bit of physical intimacy. How a boy pled his case, how his date responded, and the future of the pair as a couple depended not only on the boy's sense of his investment and the girl's scale of values, but also on the public commitment each was willing to make to the other and their tastes for emotional intimacy.[10]

Petting, that delicate standoff between sensual indulgence and constraint, was almost universal in the sense that all daters petted at some time, but not in the sense that all couples petted. Graduated physical intimacy became an accepted part of lasting teen relationships, both a marker of affection and a spur to increased commitment.

Boys were assumed to be always on the lookout for some petting, but girls were assumed on the whole to get far less physical pleasure from the act itself.[11] Boys pursued; girls rewarded boys who were affectionate, restrained, and provided a pleasant time; girls rewarded boys moderately. Even when girls were fond of petting, they found that their peer group, curiously aided by boy gossip, stood in the way of their being too easy. Even for girls in love, peer pressure set limits to lovemaking. Thus, a high school girl noted in 1929: "The girl who permits liberties is certainly popular with boys, but her popularity never lasts very long with any one boy. You know the saying, 'Just a toy to play with, not the kind they choose to grow old and grey with.'"[12] Boys' behavior could be modified: "Even freshmen girls know . . . that a boy who considers himself a gentlemen may have standards that vary according to those of the girl with whom he may be," wrote a high school dean of women.[13] Dating, thus, operated still within a double standard of sexual conduct that demanded of girls the strength to say

---

[10] Waller, describing dating at the Pennsylvania State University, far more cynically and simplistically characterized the date as incorporating mutual exploitation, with prestige and "thrills" in view (*The Family*, chap. 9; "The Rating and Dating Complex").

[11] For a classic expression of this belief see "A High School Boy Reveals Youth's Love Problems," *True Confessions* 12 (July, 1928): 34.

[12] Quoted in Arthur Dean, "A Survey on Petting," *Journal of Education* 110 (1929): 414.

[13] Jessie E. Gibson, *On Being a Girl* (New York: Macmillan, 1927), p. 141.

no and the strength of mind to prevent matters from coming to such a pass.

The absolute good girl–bad girl dichotomy inherent in this code was shifted to permit more physical expression by girls, but if blurred somewhat, it was not eradicated. Dating was threatening to girls, even as it partially liberated their heterosexual expressiveness. With imperfect contraceptive knowledge, pregnancy was a lurking danger, certainly in view of the widespread assumption that sexual excitement was rapidly progressive for inexperienced girls as well as boys. "In that first, burning kiss Betty forgot everything except that Jack was her man, her mate, her lover," *True Confessions* reported in its first volume, and steadily thereafter.[14]

The terms of the dating exchange were widely understood among the young, but not uniformly. Petting was particularly often at the heart of misunderstanding, probably because it incorporated a partial revision of the deeply inculcated double standard.[15] Certain adolescents, like "Miss Dateless," found themselves essentially outside of the dating pool because they failed or refused to recognize that this fundamental exchange in dating was normatively governed and structured by a sense of the emotions appropriate to age and stage.

> I am 20 years old and, to use the slang expression, "hard up for dates." I am rather small, but have my share of good looks. I am inevitably cheerful, like sports of all kinds and like to talk of them. I am interested in good music. . . . But—I sit at home without the boys. I think one of the reasons is that I am not common enough. I let a boy know it if he gets fresh with me and scratch him off my list. I use cosmetics, but sometimes look pale near some of these "clowns." However, they get "dates."[16]

Miss Dateless quite correctly blames her peer group for her unfortunate situation and expresses an alienation (carried by her use of the

[14] "The Danger Period," *True Confessions* 1 (August, 1922): 46.

[15] The classic 1920s' exposition is Phyllis Blanchard and Carolyn Manasses' *New Girls for Old* (New York: The Macaulay Co., 1930). Theodore Newcomb's thoughtful conclusion that by the 1930s a "less compulsive and more spontaneous demonstration of affection between boys and girls" was common suggests the gradual accomplishment of this cultural change ("Recent Changes in Attitudes toward Sex and Marriage," *American Sociological Review* 2 [1937]: 662.

[16] "Miss Dateless" to Martha Carr, "In My Opinion," *St. Louis Post-Dispatch*, October 31, 1931. And see the exchange between Doris Blake and H. Ann and Peggy, "Doris Blake's Love Answers," *New York Daily News*, October 28 and November 27, 1930. On

class term "common" and by her snide reference to "clowns") that hardly admits of much room for improvement. Letters from casualties of the dating system to lovelorn columnists are filled with evidence that they were condemned by their peers as "stuck up." Others, no doubt, simply petted, either out of anguish at being outsiders or out of anxiety at datelessness leading to matelessness. Dating, insofar as it encouraged at least somewhat spontaneous behavior in the negotiation that lay at its core, laid a cruel burden on those who were stiff and uncomfortable on dates—boy and girl alike, but more terrifyingly for girls because marriage was prescriptive for them. So also the impecunious boy and the ugly girl must suffer.

The remarkable (if problematic)[17] sexual histories collected by Al-

---

the centrality of petting, see Robert S. Lynd and Helen Merrell Lynd, *Middletown*, (New York: Harcourt, Brace, 1929), pp. 162–64.

[17] For a thorough discussion of the statistical drawbacks to the Kinsey data, see the report of a committee appointed by the American Statistical Association: William G. Cochran et al., *Statistical Problems of the Kinsey Report on Sexual Behavior of the Human Male* (Washington: American Statistical Association, 1954). On the interviewing technique, see Alfred C. Kinsey, Wardell B. Pomeroy, and Clyde E. Martin, *Sexual Behavior in the Human Male* (Philadelphia: W. B. Saunders Company, 1948), chaps. 3–4, and Kinsey et al., *Sexual Behavior in the Human Female* (Philadelphia: W. B. Saunders Company, 1953), chap. 2. On theoretical assumptions, see Paul A. Robinson, *The Modernization of Sex* (New York: Harper & Row, 1976), chap. 2. For sample, interview, and the preparation of the public-use data tape, see Paul H. Gebhard and Alan B. Johnson, *The Kinsey Data: Marginal Tabulations of the 1938–1963 Interviews* (Philadelphia: W. B. Saunders Company, 1979), which includes tabulations of all variables separately for college and noncollege white males and females and for college black males and females. Dr. Gebhard was more than courteous in permitting me to use the galleys of this volume in making up the data tape I have used and in facilitating preparation of the tape.

I here treat the white informants only; there are too few blacks to treat separately, and to merge them would merely add to the heterogeneity of the sample without (because of the high degree of education of the blacks) adding to its representativeness. I have also excluded all never-married persons from tabulations presented here, in order to avoid very thorny problems in the sexual-career sequence data, related to the vast difference between the never-married (who are considerably over-sampled by Kinsey) and those who had married, and because (as Kinsey found) sexual careers typically accelerate as marriage approaches, quite apart from age-related effects. Obviously, my decision limits the use of these samples for estimating population parameters, but homogenizes the sample in a way that relationships of variable to variable can be seen more clearly. The data presented here use all married informants born before 1910 to represent those who went through adolescence before about 1920, and those born 1910–1919 to represent the first dating cohort of adolescents. The ideal cutoff date would have been a bit earlier, but because I wished to integrate the tabular materials created for the pur-

fred Kinsey and his associates permit us a close view of the historical role of this particular dynamic of the dating system. These data point to a distinct sexualization of noncoital (or precoital) relations between the pre–World War I and postwar adolescent cohorts—more striking, indeed, than the often remarked increase in premarital coitus also recorded. Among the men and women in the ever-married sample I employed, the 34 percent of women who achieved orgasm in petting in the older cohort increased to 60 percent among the first cohort that passed its adolescence in the "dating" era; for men, the increase was from an already high 64 percent to 71 percent. The particular datum— related closely to that on orgasm—that I will employ in my discussion is age at first petting. The Kinsey data here point to an increase from 29 percent to 43 percent of girls who petted "young" (before sixteen) and an increase from 41 percent of boys to 51 percent.

Dating (and petting), I have argued, was part of a new bargain between girls and boys, weakening parents' oversight but not resolving the asymmetries implied by the double standard. Early petters among the Kinsey respondents relatively often paid the price in family tension. Table 1 indicates that while perhaps one in five of the postwar adolescent cohort recalled tension with both of his or her parents during early adolescence,[18] the proportion was markedly higher (especially for the girls) among the early petters and lower among the late petters. The pattern was absent in the earlier cohort. The reason for the historical emergence of this pattern lies in the meaning of petting to 1920s' adolescents: it was at once a source of pleasure, a coin in the dating bargain, and a challenge to parental values. In participating in the dating system, boys and girls helped modify the existing pattern of values, giving more play to preference and less to received wisdom. Parents, rightly, recognized a behavior that bespoke a larger resistance to their authority and resented it.

For peers, too, petting was increasingly incorporated into a nor-

---

poses of this paper with other work I am doing with these data, I stuck to the 1910 date I had earlier established. Clearly, I am pointing to the nature and direction of change, not trying to present accurate measurements of any given behavior for the entire population.

[18] In my tabulations, this group included those respondents who answered other than "well" to *both* questions, "When you were 14 to 17, how did you get along with your father?" and ". . . with your mother?"

TABLE 1. Proportions Reporting Conflict with Both Parents, by Sex, Cohort, and Age First Began Petting

Cohort	Petted before 14 (N)	Petted 14–15 (N)	Petted 16–17 (N)	Petted 18 or older (N)
Women				
Born before 1910	18.5%	29.6%	17.0%	19.1%
	(53)	(162)	(212)	(309)
Born 1910–1919	31.3	25.0	26.5	14.1
	(96)	(212)	(260)	(170)
Men				
Born before 1910	16.4	14.6	23.0	18.0
	(116)	(191)	(187)	(250)
Born 1910–1919	28.4	19.0	17.4	16.6
	(141)	(226)	(201)	(151)

SOURCE: Kinsey Sex Histories (ever-married whites only). See footnote 17.

matively relevant set of behaviors. To a far greater degree than parental disapproval, popularity with opposite-sex friends came to depend on comfort in petting and dating. Table 2 takes age at first petting as a crude reflection of being at ease with the evolved rules of the dating system and shows a striking relationship between such an easy accommodation and respondents' estimates of "how many (opposite-sex) friends and companions did you have . . . when you were 16 or 17." It is obviously impossible to sort out the direction of causality here: those who had petted were probably the more successful daters and possessed the qualities that made for popularity; those who were popular had the opportunity to pet. But there is no need to sort out the cause: the point is to note that in the dating era the relationship obtained for both boys and girls.

Popularity, as successful dating, depended not on particular attributes so much as on the ability to perform comfortably and enthusiastically within the peer group. When students selected their "most popular" peers (and in the "Senior Hall of Fame" compilations I have examined, "most popular" is always the honor atop the list), boys and girls adjudged "best looking," "classiest," "cutest," or "smartest" rarely

TABLE 2. Proportions Reporting "Many" Friends of the Opposite Sex at
16 or 17, by Sex, Cohort, and Age First Began Petting

Cohort	Petted before 14	Petted 14–15	Petted 16–17	Petted 18 or older
Women				
Born before 1910	64.1%	61.7%	44.5%	32.5%
Born 1910–1919	69.4	59.8	41.7	20.8
Men				
Born before 1910	49.2	41.3	30.8	14.7
Born 1910–1919	57.0	48.6	32.6	13.0

SOURCE: Kinsey Sex Histories (ever-married whites only).

were voted "most popular."[19] ("Most Studious" students never were.) Instead, the winners were outstandingly "courteous," "generous," and "thoughtful," were "busy looking," "100 per cent," filled with "class spirit," and just plain "best all-around." My sources do not reveal what derisory terms were applied to those who most apparently lacked such social ease. We can, however, be sure that for them the oversight of courtship by peers seemed a poor substitute for the parental role that had been abandoned.

The only serious historical account of the emergence of the dating system is that of the historian Paula Fass, whose recent *The Damned and the Beautiful* is a subtle view of the youth culture that emerged among collegians in the 1920s. Fass interprets dating as one among many of the accomplishments of a self-conscious generation, acting in part over and against its predecessors: "It was not caprice . . . that made them question traditional proprieties in sexual morality and in such areas as smoking, drinking, and dancing. These the young defined as the private sector, as a sphere for personal expression to be governed by need and taste rather than by law and morals. . . . The young knew that their patterns and attitudes provided a margin of dif-

[19] *Minneapolis Central High News*, April 26 and December 20, 1923; April 20, 1926; April 27, 1927. For contemporaneous confirmation of the centrality of such traits to popularity among high school–age children see the correlation matrices of personality traits in Caroline McCann Tyron, *Evaluations of Adolescent Personality By Adolescents*, monograph of the Society for Research in Child Development, vol. 4, no. 4 (Washington: National Research Council, 1939), chap. 2.

ference between them and their elders, and gave them a vehicle for group cohesion."[20]

Oddly, perhaps inadvertently, Fass's explanation of dating in the 1920s abandons internal group factors for such macrosocial factors as mobility, commercial amusement, and an overall weakening of family authority. Moreover, while I find her description of the dating scene most persuasive and the notion of self-conscious youth compelling, two elements in her account demand reconsideration. First, her identification of youth with collegians leads her to overlook the fact that a dating system evolved simultaneously among high school students. This part of the system affected more people and coincided with the period of heterosexual awakening in participants' lives. Second, the generality of Fass's account of youth probably explains her mistaken assumption of a basic unity of interest within middle-class youth that denies that boys and girls had different things at stake in the development of dating.

Fass powerfully demonstrates that the symbols of generational revolt were preeminently borne by women and that they took the form of the narrowing of the differences in the behaviors of the two genders: language, clothing, smoking, hairstyle, and social intercourse between the sexes, in the latter constituting a modest challenge to the double standard of sexual propriety.[21] If "freedom" or autonomy seemed to contemporaries to be at stake, in retrospect, youth—and young women in particular—seem to have proposed no fundamental changes in the moral order, only the lifting of limitations, based on age and gender, upon their own right to choose among conventional options. They challenged received definitions of authority, not morality, positioning themselves to take advantage of the alluring but hardly revolutionary range of new consumer choice created by the burgeoning economy.[22] If

[20] Paula S. Fass, *The Damned and the Beautiful* (New York: Oxford University Press, 1979), pp. 262–63, 324–25. Elsewhere, more persuasively, she explains other facets of youth behavior in the 1920s by group characteristics of youth, notably its segregation, enhanced material endowment, and institutional completeness.

[21] Ibid.

[22] Choice, wide and frequent, had come to dominate considerations of quality and price in consumer behavior. See, for example, Paul H. Nystrom, *Fashion Merchandising* (New York: The Ronald Press, 1932), p. 31. On the morally unsettling impact of consumer choice as proposed by "the passing show" of luxury and fashion, see William I. Thomas, *The Unadjusted Girl* (1923; reprint ed., New York: Harper Torchbook, 1967), p. 82. And, on the kinds of dilemmas radically enlarged choice posed for modern young

sex was now "as frankly discussed as automobiles or the advantage of cold storage over moth balls, why should our elders consider our interest in this subject a sign of unnaturalness or perversion? Should it not constitute the chief concern of those in whose hands the future generation lies?"[23] If young people in rejecting received courtship procedures rejected traditional romanticism, they by no means rejected marriage or marriage based on love.[24] The dating system, as they understood it, was an institutional framework to accomplish exactly this end.

The dating system suited boys well, but its establishment represented some inroads upon the double standard. The main architects of its code were girls.[25] Before dating, parents tended to construe strictly girls' obligation to enter marriage untainted by even a hint of scandal, and they supervised courting accordingly, limiting not only its occasion, but, to a degree, the set of eligibles. The boy who came calling had not only to be prepared to behave himself; he also had to pass prima facie muster as a boy who by reputation *would* behave himself. Under the double standard, however, boys' reputations were both subject to repair and of far less interest to their own families. Whereas girls had to be chosen by a boy and then gain parental permission to receive his attentions, boys had only to choose. The girls had more to gain by the establishment of dating, because the new version of the double standard that it put in place was considerably less restrictive to them than the one it replaced.

II

In the 1920s, as Fass argues, "the schools first and foremost gave youth a setting and a home, . . . [where] the society of peers flourished, enclosing the young in a world that was theirs by right of possession."

---

people (especially girls), see Margaret Mead, "Adolescence in Primitive and Modern Society," in *The New Generation*, ed. V. F. Calverton and Samuel D. Schmalhausen (New York: The Macaulay Co., 1930), pp. 169–88.

[23] Regina Malone, "Has Youth Deteriorated? II: The Fabulous Monster," *The Forum* 76 (1926): 29.

[24] See, for example, Ernest R. Burgess, "The Romantic Impulse and Family Disorganization," *Survey* 57 (1926): 290–94; Alexander Black, "Is the Young Person Coming Back?" *Harper's Monthly* 149 (1929): 337–46; and, for the parents' perspective, see Jessica H. Cosgrave, "Romantic Love," *Good Housekeeping* 81 (November–December, 1928): 36.

[25] The girls who did not prosper under the new system shortly became its victims. As

Fass particularly intends to describe residential colleges, maintaining by a comparison that "the world of the high school was more circumscribed by adult supervision and regulation; . . . in the high school the peer group was one of a number of competing influences."[26] There is some truth to this, but Fass has not really looked at much high school evidence, and this points to a fully elaborated dating system. Moreover, high school rather than college included the ages at which boys and girls started seeking each other out.[27] It is a trifle difficult to imagine young people practicing parentally supervised "courting" through the high school years, but then regearing themselves emotionally for dating in college. And while we must grant Fass's important point about the relative strength of peer-group dominance at college as compared with high school, the high school subjected far more young people to an age-graded setting and encouraged the kind of peer-group activities that (as Fass suggests) created a controllable leadership structure among the students.[28]

The middle of the teenage spectrum rather than either end was most implicated in the sharp expansion of schooling in the 1920s smack in the middle of the high school years. The graph, comparing the proportion of unmarried boys and girls who attended school during 1920 and 1930, shows the focus of the expansion to be among sixteen- and seventeen-year-olds, for both sexes.[29] To be sure, college grew even more explosively than did high schooling in the 1920s in proportional

---

early as 1924, a California high school dean of girls set up a program to help those girls (54 percent in her school, by her reckoning) who were left out. There were many reasons for failure, "yet it will be observed that all of these various types have something in common. The non-social individual centers all her thoughts and activity upon herself." (Note the contrast with the traits of the popular girl.) See Caroline Power, "The Social Program for the Unsocial High-School Girl," *School Review* 32 (1924): 773.

[26] Fass, *The Damned*, pp. 129, 211. But see the small-town ethnography of "Age-Group Conflict and Our Changing Culture," by Earl H. Bell, a University of Nebraska sociologist, in *Social Forces* 12 (1933): 237–43. Bell casually drops the phrase "the period of dating and high school" (p. 238).

[27] Phyllis Blanchard, *The Adolescent Girl* (New York: Moffat, Yard and Company, 1920).

[28] A persuasive ethnographic account of high school as "a fairly complete social cosmos in itself" is found in Lynd and Lynd, *Middletown*, p. 211, and in chap. 6 generally.

[29] I have assumed that almost no one was both married and attending school, which 1930 data suggest was quite the case. Eliminating the married directs our attention to the youth at risk of dating. Data are from the *Population: General Reports* volumes of the 1920 and 1930 U.S. censuses.

terms. Between 1920 and 1930, B.A.s conferred increased by 152 percent while the number of high school diplomas awarded grew by a
somewhat more modest 114 percent. In both college and high school
the sex ratio of graduates evened out during the decade, women collegians approaching the number of men, boy high school graduates
nearly equalling girls. Trends aside, colleges still enrolled and graduated far more men than women, but high schools had almost even sex
ratios—a demography far more conducive to widespread dating than
that in college.[30] Many college men had to import female companions
("townies"), whom they often sought to exploit sexually as "bad girls,"
in a setting lacking the near equality and peer group oversight of the
evolving high school date, thereby emphasizing rather than mitigating
the double standard.[31]

In the 1920s, age homogenization was a self-conscious policy of
many high school administrators, accomplished even as the schools expanded rapidly and took in students from families that were close
enough to the economic margin to require supplementary income from
their children from time to time.[32] Nonpromotion increasingly was
seen to encourage dropping out, and this seen as unfortunate; "social
promotion" now suited educational and developmental theory. (Early
promotion was far less common.) A dramatic example of the progress of
age homogenization is found in the school system of Duluth, Minnesota. Among sixteen-year-olds attending Duluth public schools in
1920–1921, only 25.1 percent of the boys and 36.1 percent of the girls
were in a single grade; five years of age homogenization brought these
figures to 33.5 percent and 40.2 percent; by the mid-1930s they were

[30] Note Waller's discussion of the relationship of sex ratio to exploitative dating in
"Rating and Dating."

[31] The operation of this structure is acutely explored in Winston Ehrmann, *Premarital Dating Behavior* (New York: Holt, 1959), pp. 143–62. For a review of dating in colleges in the 1920s, see R. H. Edwards, J. M. Artman, and Galen M. Fisher, *Under-
graduates: A Study of Morale in Twenty-Three American Colleges and Universities*
(Garden City, N.Y.: Doubleday, Doran, 1928), chap. 5.

[32] John K. Folger and Charles B. Nam, *Education of the American Population*, 1960
Census Monographs (Washington: U.S. Government Printing Office, 1967), pp. 8–9.
For a fine, naive, contemporaneous expression of recent changes as they affected school
life, see Olivia Pound, "The Social Life of High School Girls: Its Problems and Its Opportunities," *School Review* 28 (1920): 50–56. On economic aspects of school prolongation,
see Howard G. Burdge, *Our Boys* (Albany: State of New York, Military Training Commission, Bureau of Vocational Training, 1921), chaps. 13, 23.

GRAPH I
PROPORTIONS OF NEVER-MARRIED BOYS AND GIRLS
ATTENDING SCHOOL, BY SINGLE YEAR OF AGE 1920 AND 1930

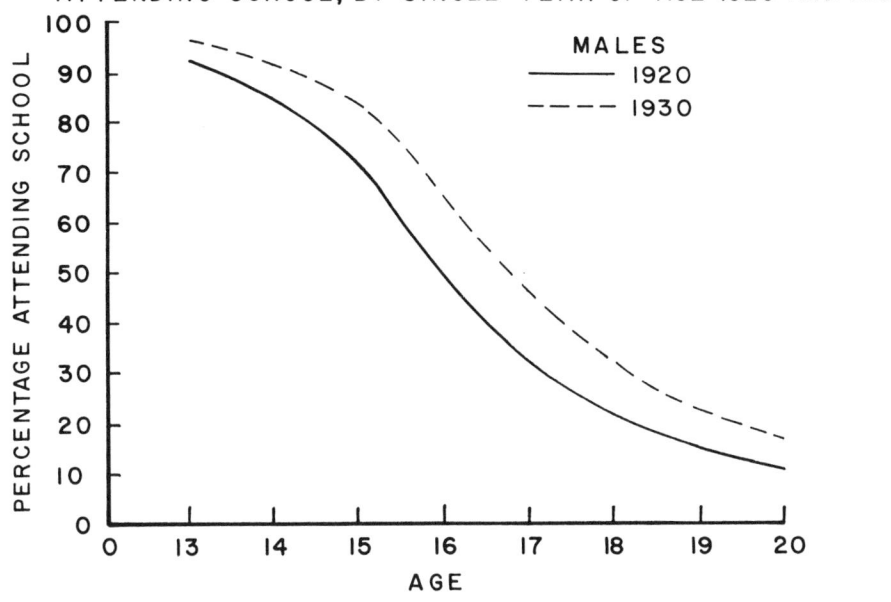

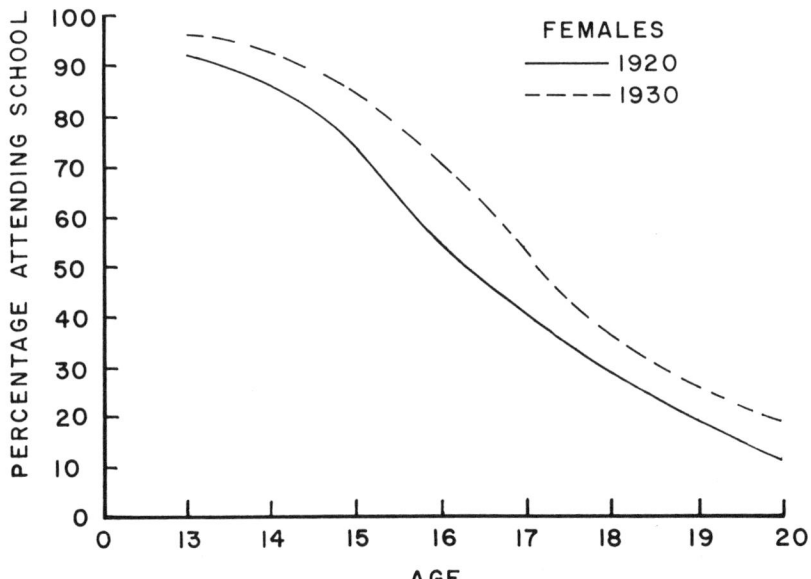

SOURCE: U.S. Census of Population, 1920 and 1930

up to 41.6 percent and 54.2 percent.[33] (The continued greater age homogenization of girls is explained by their greater trained capacity for
regimentation, as at school, and by the greater pressure for boys to
earn money.) Homogenization by age makes a great deal of difference
to dating, since dating depended upon freely entered short-term agree-
ments between near equals, differentiated mainly by gender, and over-
seen by the opinion of mutually valued, interrelated sets of age peers.
Age, with its correlated experience, earning capacity, and prestige was
the kind of differentiator that could render too unequal the negotiation
at dating's core. (In parallel with cultural expectations governing marriage, girls could date somewhat older boys.) Age homogenization limited exploitation and permitted the girls to move somewhat beyond the
constrictive safety provided by adherence to the double standard.

The formal extracurricular life of the high school quickly came to be
articulated with the interpersonal dynamics of the dating system.
Quite early, many high schools instituted dances, in an effort of varying
success to take the play away from commercial dance halls and road
houses.[34] Too, "it is a well-known fact that club pins are an absolute
necessity when a young man wishes to plight his time-enduring regard
for some lady, but, even considering this, it ought not be necessary to
have more than three or four."[35] Beyond visible symbols, word of
mouth was powerful where everybody was likely to know everybody.
"Why should we have so many idle gossipers in the school? . . . Much
to our dislike we have many social groups and this lowers cooperation
within the student body."[36] Gossip, of course, while lowering cooperation also regulated behavior—reassuringly for the most part, op-
pressively upon occasion. Trends in fashion were sharply defined and
served to mark out those who qualified for the dating pool. A "bobbed
hair census" at Little Falls (Minnesota) High in 1923 indicated the

[33] Duluth, Board of Education, *Annual Report*, 1921, 1926, 1937. In New Bedford,
Massachusetts, in 1922, only 21 percent of sixteen-year-old boys were found in a single
grade, and only 26 percent of the girls; by 1930 these figures had increased to 38 and 39
percent, respectively. (New Bedford, *School Report*, 1923, 1931).

[34] Ella Gardner, *Public Dance Halls* (U.S. Department of Labor, Children's Bureau,
Publication No. 189, 1929), pp. 36–49; and see M. V. O'Shea, *The Trend of the Teens*
(Chicago: Frederick S. Drake and Co., 1920).

[35] Editorial, *St. Paul Central High Times*, December 16, 1927. And see *Minneapolis
South High Southerner*, April 13, 1921, letter from A.C.

[36] *Little Falls The Comet's Tail*, February 24, 1928, editorial. Also see Lynd and
Lynd, *Middletown*, pp. 162–64.

strength of fashion: in each of the four classes, more than three girls in four adopted this hair style, so rich in affirmation of modernity.[37] (Even among "sub-freshmen," 65 percent had already caught on.)

I do not propose even to speculate about when the institution of dating began. The records of behavior initiated by children are as spotty as for any literate group, and an institution that "just grew" found no chroniclers, much as it provides few pegs for the memory. Adolescent diaries for the twentieth century are surely not rare, but do not seem to be collected. What is documentable is that the elaboration of dating as a system began in the first quarter of the current century and spread with noteworthy rapidity from an initially urban and middle-class epicenter during the 1920s and 1930s. The circumstances of youth itself provide one key to this timing, as does also the rapid enlargement of consumer choice. An ideological element, too, played a part. The frankly—if guardedly—sexual quality of the date (and thereby of courtship incorporating the date) is consistent with "proper" behavior for boys and girls only after "the conspiracy of silence" governing sexual matters was challenged in the public areas and some consequences of the double standard of sexual morality called into question by highly respectable twentieth-century reformers and symbolically challenged by "new women."[38]

Dating spread remarkably quickly. In a San Jose, California, high school, two-thirds of the sophomore boys and three-quarters of senior boys were dating in 1930. Data collected in 1933 from a large sample of high school girls, oversampled among Catholic schools, found that half of the freshmen and 84 percent of the seniors had begun dating. An excellent study of an urban high school found that in 1941 virtually every boy had dated by his senior year, and all but 14 percent of the girls.[39] Burgess and Wallin presented data collected mainly from col-

[37] *Little Falls The Comet's Tail*, March 27, 1923.

[38] John C. Burnham, "The Progressive Era Revolution in American Attitudes toward Sex," *Journal of American History* 59 (1973): 885–909; Mark Thomas Connelly, *The Response to Prostitution in the Progressive Era* (Chapel Hill: University of North Carolina Press, 1980).

[39] In the San Jose study, only 30 percent of the senior boys dated as often as once a week. See Frederick T. Shipp, "Social Activities of High-School Boys," *School Review* 39 (1931): 771; Sister M. Mildred Knoebber, "The Adolescent Girl" (Ph.D. dissertation, St. Louis University, 1935), p. 162; Helen Moore Priester, "The Reported Dating Practices of One Hundred and Six High School Seniors in an Urban Community" (M.A. essay, Cornell University, 1941), p. 41.

lege students and graduates, pertaining to the late 1920s and early 1930s, which indicates that about one-third of both boys and girls dated by age fourteen, a bit more than two-thirds by sixteen, and virtually all by eighteen. A national, "faithfully balanced cross-section of high school students" in 1942 gave average estimates of 71 percent of the boys and 63 percent of the girls "necking" on dates, averaged over the four years of high school.[40]

Dating is almost universally identified as an urban pattern in its early years and not a rural one. A careful study of upstate New York rural girls in 1933 revealed that although the institution had definitely made its way into the countryside, it had done so rather tenuously. Thirty-three percent of the girls aged fifteen to seventeen had never yet dated, and an additional 49 percent did not yet date "consistently." Even at ages eighteen to twenty, 58 percent were not yet consistent daters, in addition to the 15 percent who still did not date at all. It is noteworthy that for each younger cohort of girls interviewed, dating had begun younger, as the institution diffused, but at the mid-30s alternative modes of mate selection were still in operation in the country.[41] These girls, when they dated, went to movies, dances, parties, and on motor rides, just as did urban youth. But where the rural families were less prosperous than families in upstate New York, rural social life devoted exclusively to youth was exceptionally truncated. In the countryside, parents' capacity to exercise close supervision was often too great; many farm youth were even said to seek the city partly on this account. Urbanites brought up on the dating system described as "grim" the marriage that a farm girl might contract without "a chance to get out when she was a girl, to know more men," to find through dating "the singing joy that lightens daily burdens."[42]

[40] Ernest W. Burgess and Paul Wallin, *Engagement and Marriage* (Philadelphia: Lippincott, 1953), p. 119; "The Fortune Survey," *Fortune* 26 (December, 1942). Almost identical findings for a somewhat similar sample are reported in John C. Flanagan, "A Study of Factors Determining Family Size in a Selected Professional Group," *Genetic Psychology Monographs* 25 (1942): 78.

[41] Mildred B. Thurow, "Interests, Activities, and Problems of Rural Young Folk: I," in *Bulletin 617* (Ithaca, N.Y.: Cornell University Agricultural Experiment Station, 1934): 34.

[42] Paul H. Landis, "Problems of Farm Youth—A Point of View," *Social Forces* 18 (1940): 502–13; O. Latham Hatcher, *Rural Girls in the City for Work* (Richmond, Va.: Garrett and Massie for the Southern Women's Educational Alliance, 1930), pp. 52–53; "Dearly Desired," *True Romances* (March, 1941): 20.

Urban working-class youth seem to have had sufficient distance from parental oversight to erect a dating system, but other matters militated against it. Jane Synge's fine oral history accounts of family life during this period in Hamilton, Ontario, indicate that for working-class daughters parental oversight often extended no further than the initial permission to be called upon by the first boy or two. Thereafter, perhaps, courtships might ensue that were strangely "informal" and without recognizable stages: "Direct control was impossible since . . . most informants met their spouses-to-be at work and spent time with them on the way to and from work."[43] Yet working-class children could not control the time, place, or tempo of such contacts. They also lacked both the wherewithal for the "good time" dating asked of the boy and the effective, school-based, same-age peer group that oversaw behavior within the dating system. The sociological accounts of Donovan on waitresses, Thrasher on the boy gang, and Thomas on girl delinquents discuss nonmiddle-class milieus of the 1920s lacking in both material wherewithal and overseeing peer groups, in which dating in the sense we are discussing clearly does not organize heterosexual contact.[44] Whyte's Boston observations in the mid-1930s pointed out the continued existence of ethnic working-class settings in which assumptions about gender roles rendered dating inappropriate.[45] Even among less isolated high school students, impecunious boys operated at a real disadvantage in the dating system, a problem that was to become acute during the Depression, since the terms of the date still required the boy to *purchase* amusement for the couple.[46] In college, the "economic

[43] Jane Synge, "The Way We Were: Farm and City Families in the Early Twentieth Century" (Unpublished manuscript, Department of Sociology, McMaster University, Hamilton, Ontario, n.d.), chap. 5 (quoted here by permission of the author).

[44] Frances Donovan, *The Woman Who Waits* (Boston: Richard G. Badger, 1920), chaps. 17–19; Frederic M. Thrasher, *The Gang* (Chicago: University of Chicago Press, 1927), chap. 13; Thomas, *Unadjusted Girl*, chap. 3.

[45] William Foote Whyte, "A Slum Sex Code," *American Journal of Sociology* 49 (1943): 24–29; and see Dorothy Reed, *Leisure Time of Girls in a "Little Italy"* (Portland, Oregon: Privately printed, 1932; Ph.D. dissertation, Columbia University, n.d.).

[46] Emory S. Bogardus, *The City Boy and His Problems* (Los Angeles: Rotary Club of Los Angeles, 1926), pp. 44–45; Bell, "Age-Group Conflict," pp. 240–41; Nettie Pauline McGill and Ellen Nathalie Matthews, *The Youth of New York City* (New York: Macmillan, 1940), p. 315; Rachel Stutsman, *What of Youth Today?* (Detroit: Detroit Youth Study Committee, 1935), Table 28. In a peculiar way, some affectionate couples were pressed by Depression shortfalls toward a substitution of intimacy for amusement—that is, toward the substitution of a different kind of arrangement for the dating negotiation:

status" of boys (but not of girls) explained more than "looks" about how young they started dating, how often they dated, and how intimate they became with their dating partner. Girls, of course, needed to spend at least enough to keep up with clothing fashions.[47]

By the end of the Depression decade, dating was generally but not entirely diffused as a youth pattern and as an aspect of mate selection. The dating system was part of a larger set of behaviors in which youthful peer groups arrogated authority previously exercised by adults within the family. A remarkable youth survey conducted in 1939 asked about several of these symbolic areas of conduct (although, unfortunately, not very directly about dating), permitting us a suggestive view of the bounds of the youth culture at this date.[48]

Table 3 makes evident, first of all, that in 1939 both smoking (as an example) and differing with parents about opposite-sex friends were strongly dependent upon both age and gender. Large proportions of

---

"The boy I love doesn't come to see me any more because he hasn't any money. All I want is him." Dorothy to Doris Blake, *New York Daily News*, November 27, 1930.

[47]Robert F. Winch, "Interrelations between Certain Social Background and Parent-Son Factors in a Study of Courtship among College Men," *American Sociological Review* 11 (1946): 335; idem, "Courtship in College Women," *American Journal of Sociology* 55 (1949): 273. A student protested that girls' excessive dependence upon fashion leaders had antidemocratic implications: "In the grade schools perhaps the difference in dress is not noted, but when a girl enters high school she is thrown in contact with girls of her classes who use the classroom as sort of a 'style show.' Many girls have left school because their parents were not able to dress them well enough to 'keep up' with the more fortunate few" (*Minneapolis West High Weekly*, April 11, 1919). And see Lynd and Lynd, *Middletown*, 162–64.

[48]The Youth Survey, August, 1939, is Roper Commercial Poll No. 15, and is available at the archives of the Roper Center, University of Connecticut. The sponsor of the survey was the National Tea Bureau, a trade group that evidently sought to inquire into youth's attitudes toward tea drinking and how these fit into what we would call the youth culture. The questionnaire is rich in material on "reference groups" and on relationships with parents. For present purposes, we focus on just two items. Roughly equal numbers of boys and girls at each age and roughly equal numbers of children at each year of age ten through nineteen were questioned in the survey, 3,139 altogether. I have excluded children under fourteen from the tabulations presented here as not germane to my inquiry and omitted those without clear answers to the questions tabulated. A memo from an Elmo Roper employee, dated 1968, in the Roper Center archives indicates that "most nationwide samples at that time were of the quota-type," with the quotas for age, sex, geographic distribution, and size of place. This indicates that the sample is not suitable for estimating national population parameters, but that relationships of variables are credible, which is what I seek. Note that the discussion here relates group-level not individual-level patterns.

TABLE 3. Smoking and Conflict with Parents over Opposite-sex Friends by Sex and Age, by Father's Occupational Category, and by Town Size, 1939

	Boys			Girls		
	14–15	16–17	18–19	14–15	16–17	18–19
Group	(N)	(N)	(N)	(N)	(N)	(N)
Smoke regularly or occasionally (All)	23.6%	44.8%	66.0%	9.0%	21.0%	44.2%
	(314)	(306)	(300)	(312)	(310)	(303)
Father's occupational type						
White collar	16.1	37.4	64.8	12.2	31.5	64.8
	(112)	(115)	(128)	(123)	(127)	(125)
Blue collar	23.1	45.5	71.3	3.9	11.3	27.8
	(136)	(134)	(101)	(128)	(115)	(97)
Farm	31.1	55.3	63.2	10.0	25.6	21.1
	(45)	(38)	(57)	(40)	(39)	(57)
Town size						
1 million +	26.2	52.2	62.8	0.0	12.8	74.4
	(42)	(46)	(43)	(40)	(39)	(43)
25,000–999,999	15.1	31.7	72.3	12.4	30.2	56.1
	(86)	(82)	(83)	(89)	(86)	(82)
Town to 24,999	21.9	37.1	49.2	11.0	21.3	42.6
	(73)	(70)	(63)	(73)	(75)	(68)
Rural	30.1	56.5	72.1	8.2	16.4	24.5
	(113)	(108)	(111)	(110)	(110)	(110)
"Have different ideas from either one or both of your parents on (girl) (boy) friends" (All)	12.9	16.0	21.5	29.6	39.4	42.0
	(310)	(301)	(298)	(314)	(307)	(298)
Father's occupational type						
White collar	9.0	11.4	21.3	29.0	37.3	42.7
	(111)	(114)	(127)	(124)	(126)	(124)
Blue collar	15.7	19.4	23.3	25.6	36.8	39.6
	(134)	(134)	(103)	(129)	(114)	(96)
Farm	22.2	14.3	19.6	41.5	55.1	46.4
	(45)	(35)	(56)	(41)	(49)	(56)

TABLE 3. (continued)

Group	Boys			Girls		
	14–15 (N)	16–17 (N)	18–19 (N)	14–15 (N)	16–17 (N)	18–19 (N)
Town size						
1 million +	7.3	15.2	11.4	23.1	30.0	36.6
	(41)	(46)	(44)	(39)	(40)	(41)
25,000–999,999	16.3	9.8	26.2	31.1	32.1	36.6
	(86)	(82)	(80)	(90)	(84)	(82)
Town to 24,999	8.6	20.3	23.8	24.7	40.0	41.2
	(70)	(69)	(63)	(73)	(75)	(68)
Rural	17.7	18.3	20.7	33.9	48.1	48.6
	(113)	(104)	(111)	(112)	(108)	(107)

SOURCE: Roper Commercial Poll No. 15, Roper Center, University of Connecticut.

boys and girls eventually took up smoking as they grew up, but boys started earlier than girls and continued to smoke more commonly. While smoking was generally considered a fitting thing for young men to do in 1939, for some girls it connoted a "racier" image than they desired. If girls were more restrained than boys in adopting cigarettes as a sign of self-determination, they were nevertheless considerably more likely than boys to report conflict with their parents about such issues as opposite-sex friends. Undoubtedly, the girls' answers here reflected real differences in the closeness of the scrutiny parents attempted to exercise over their activities, dating in particular. For both boys and girls, as they grew up, the tensions over this question were exacerbated. But girls were held to a higher standard.

Among boys, smoking (at any given age) varied rather little by father's occupational type (our indicator of the class of the family) and varied little, too, by the size of town or city in which the family lived. The rapid adoption of cigarettes was essentially ubiquitous for boys. For girls, the story was different. Most striking is the class difference: really, it is fair to say that among teenage girls, smoking (and probably dating) developed first in the middle class and to a degree remained particularly a middle-class habit. Middle-class girls were pretty nearly as likely to smoke at any given age as boys. But strong gender differences were present for blue-collar and farm families, which denied girls the freedom to smoke that they granted their sons. Girls, too, but not boys, were treated differently in city and countryside. Whether they lived in large or small city, town, or countryside, boys learned to smoke according to pretty much the same schedule. Girls, however, who commonly smoked if they lived in cities, smoked only rarely if they lived on farms, with intermediate-sized places arrayed appropriately in between. It was in the large city where girls developed and enforced upon their parents a peer code that incorporated the sophisticated gesture of smoking, a gesture that even in 1939 gained meaning in part from its similarity to the behavior of the boys and in part from the contrast it allowed them to make to their parents' generation (and to rural girls). I do not doubt but much the same pattern obtained with regard to aspects of the dating code itself.

If sophistication varied systematically, as we have seen was the case with smoking, we might well hypothesize that conflict with parents (as that about opposite-sex friends) varied in the same way. We have seen this to have been the case with regard to age, but that girls at once were less free in their behavior than boys and more often at odds with their parents. Table 3 indicates, moreover, that in the places and in the social categories in which girls were more sophisticated, a *smoother* accommodation with their parents had on the whole already been accomplished. The dating system here had already realized its potential of promoting cultural change. Blue-collar and white-collar parents of girls (as of boys) were equally likely to differ with their daughters over boyfriends. Despite the different pace at which peer norms affected girls' behaviors, parents of both social classes grew concerned to roughly the same degree as their daughters grew up. Farm parents, on the other hand, kept their daughters away from smoking rather successfully, evidently by a prickly and active oversight over their social activities more generally, especially at the younger ages. Nonfarm parents had settled into a truce with their children, an uneasy one to be sure, that farm parents hadn't quite accepted yet—two decades after urban girls made gestures in the direction of what they saw as freedom. The tabulations by city size, likewise, indicate that in 1939 the further away one was from the sources of urban sophistication, the more likely was the clash of cultures between the generations.

Granted, the argument is inferential, but it seems safe to argue that a diffusion process spread the dating complex from middle to urban working-class families, and from city to countryside. For this, no doubt, we can credit the concurrent differential pace of the spread of age-homogenized high schools, the consumer culture, and "modern" values regarding sex and gender. The interrelated set of behavioral manifestations and redefinitions of personal feelings that dating entailed, permitting as they did girls to negotiate a somewhat more balanced set of gender relationships with their dates than their predecessors had received under their parents' protection, moved gradually through the American culture. One can easily imagine how a dating boy might teach a formerly nondating girl the rudiments, and how adolescent conversation could convey the essence of the institution. "Cora told me that I was a fool to high-hat Ben. He was a good, hard-working guy, she said, and would make a swell husband. But . . . I wasn't in any hurry to get married, and when I did, I wanted someone different from Ben," who was a repetitious, sexually unimaginative, and distinctly *cheap* date. In this 1931 confession, the narrator but not Cora had learned the middle-class dating code.[49]

III

Despite their substantially united front toward their parents' generation, boys and girls had by no means identical interests in the new dating scheme. The earlier female growth spurt provided a convenient sign for what contemporaries believed (and thereby encouraged) to be girls' earlier awareness of the opposite sex as objects of interest. Contemporary accounts of adolescent behavior had boys entering the high school ages still in a "gang stage," while girls had long before turned to "fancies . . . of men and boys, and of herself as the center of attraction and interest. . . . She becomes interested in dress and personal adornment . . . [and] ruin[s] her healthy skin with rouge and lipstick."[50] Girls, furthermore, more often than boys remained through high school

[49] "Play Girl of Coney Island," *True Confessions* 19 (August, 1931): 247.
[50] Winifred Richmond, *The Adolescent Girl* (1925; reprint ed., New York: Macmillan, 1936), p. 53; cf. idem, *The Adolescent Boy* (New York: Farrar and Rinehart, 1933); and for an unconventional statement of the conventional understanding on this point, see Ben B. Lindsey and Wainwright Evans, *The Revolt of Modern Youth* (New York: Boni & Liveright, 1925), chaps. 5 and 6. Lindsey and Evans hold, on p. 66, that "the high-school boy is a much less dramatic figure than the high-school girl. Generally, she sets the pace, whatever it is to be, and he dances to her piping."

graduation. If there were more girls in high school potentially to be seeking dates, so also higher proportions of them, particularly among the freshmen and sophomores, presumably hoped to date. Accordingly, girls sought to limit competition by defining its terms and to enlarge the pool of eligible boys. There was, of course, the alternative possibility for a girl to be a collegian's or an employed boy's "townie," but such a choice took the date outside its familiar negotiating balance and outside the supportive structure of peer-group gossip. Gossip and the clique system operated to limit the terms of competition among girls, most particularly by regulating the amount of physical gratification with which they could reward their dates: commonly such gossip took the form of "catty" statements that anyone could get boys by giving a good deal of sex (i.e., that this did not reflect true popularity). Meanwhile, the repeated jousting and chiding of the boy population in general (sometimes, happily for the historian, in the high school newspaper) served to bring marginal boys into the dating pool. Ritualized gender conflict was one of the most striking aspects of high school newspapers, and, one suspects, of peer-group activities more generally, when these supported the dating system.

Chiding served to educate boys to the proper ways of behaving toward girls, so that the rules of the dating system might be learned even by the more backward boys: "Boys, is it fair to make the girls come to a school entertainment unescorted? So far, I have not been to an entertainment without seeing three-fourths of the girls come without escorts. The most disgusting thing about it is, that the boys act as though they did not realize the predicament they've placed the girls in. . . . I believe the faculty should make a rule that no girls come to the parties unescorted and that no boy be admitted without a young lady."[51] Or: "What has come over the boys of this school? . . . Is it the lack of carfare? I am sure that we girls would be happy to supply that . . . instead of going home alone after 11 o'clock. Fewer girls will be allowed to attend parties at school, since they must return late alone. Just because a boy is gentleman enough to take a girl home, is no reason that he is in love with her. All we want is common courtesy, not husbands."[52] Boys must be taught the nonbinding quality of a date, to distinguish it from the courtship system that dating was replacing. The complaint was not

---

[51] L. C. in *Minneapolis South High Southerner*, February 29, 1919.
[52] "One of Them" in *Minneapolis South High Southerner*, October 27, 1920.

misdirected, for an earnest correspondent responded in the next issue: "There are many reasons. Not that the young man has not the price of carfare, or is too stingy, but that the girls of to-day are too different from those of yesterday. He has not as yet become acquainted with their ways. It will take a long time unless the girls do their part and bring the boys out of that bashful state which is keeping them from mixing in with the girls and being treated as equals. Therefore, act as though you wanted to be taken home, and I am sure you will not be disappointed."[53]

"Bashful" was the word. Throughout the decade, female correspondents in all of these papers would resurrect it as an adjective of mild condescension addressed to the boys they hoped to recruit to the pool of dating eligibles: "As usual, only senior and junior girls are to be present, but boys of the lower classes are allowed to come. In that case the senior and junior girls must wait to be invited before they can attend. It would be unfortunate to have these girls left out and, weird as it may seem, the task of inviting them is up to the boys—bashful and otherwise. Let's have as many junior and senior girls asked as possible, boys."[54] "Stags" posed a problem, and girls pressed for the elimination of stags and the establishment of fixed-partner dates at school dances and no doubt elsewhere. For girls, the "stag" arrangement and its attendant "cutting in" at dances was an invitation to humiliation or boredom and left all the power of decision making in the hands of boys, who not rarely looked after one another's interests and gave no thought to the wallflowers the system inevitably created. "Just fancy knowing that a boy is dancing past the stagline and waving a five-dollar bill behind your back as an offer to anyone who'll come and take you away!"[55] While in the dating system a girl had to wait on a boy's invitation, once an invitation was issued, a boy was bound (if imperfectly until the system was quite learned) to honor certain rules of conduct.

A correspondent to the *Minneapolis Central High News* in 1924 put the problem well: "What is a sunlite [informal daytime dance] for? Is it so the male population of the school can go and occupy one side of the room and the female population go and occupy another? There are the

[53] *Minneapolis South High Southerner*, November 18, 1920.
[54] Letter of E. D., *St. Paul Central High Times*, March 26, 1926.
[55] "We Are Bachelor Girls of 30," *True Confessions* 26 (June 1935): 38–39.

same few boys at every sunlite who won't dance—they just stand there. Why will a boy go to a girl's home and dance all evening and then not dance with her any place else? Is it that he doesn't consider her good enough? . . . May I have an answer to this question from some one of the 'Stags'?"[56] Why would some boys act in this fashion, and why would girls object to it? To understand this we need to take into consideration the ambiguous moral meaning of dancing at the time. Dancing was one of the symbols of youth revolt, and in this symbolic meaning dancing was downright sexual. But between members of a generation who had grown up with such forms, the meaning of dancing was in the main recreation and structured sociability, but inherently suggestive and potentially explosive. Boys, as a group, found it in their interest to press dancing in a sexual direction, which suited girls' purposes insofar as the dancing served as a declaration of generational freedom; but for them the sexualization of dancing also inched the terms of the boy-girl negotiation that much closer to "going too far," at which point they had more to lose. The public nature of the high school dance, accordingly—aside from fueling the competitive element of the dating system—served girls' purposes ideally. Thus, perhaps, when the Alexandria (Minnesota) High School circulated in 1927 a questionnaire to its students regarding more parties and, for the first time, school dances, both boys and girls voted overwhelmingly for more parties, but boys only split evenly on dances, which girls supported by five to two.[57]

Probably far less important to girls than their partial escape from parental oversight was the right subtly to affirm in dating the sexual element in courtship, which value they shared (if not to the same extent) with boys. But even here, girls had something special at stake, because in dating physical pleasure was defined as properly a token of affection and commitment. Through dating, girls considerably before marriage could discover with boys patterns of emotional intimacy congruent with those the female subculture had long valued, but without ultimate commitment, physical or marital.[58] Nor need the task of finding a good mate be forgotten, for the dating system elaborated a series

[56] *Minneapolis Central High News*, November 13, 1924.

[57] *Alexandria High Al-Hi-Nuz*, December 16, 1927.

[58] Fass, *The Damned*, chap. 6, is splendid on the meaning of sexuality if a little underemphatic about the gender dialectic.

of stages that led toward engagement and beyond. The tender interpersonal qualities sought in a good date, while not identical to those of
a good mate, were nevertheless among the desirable traits. For boys,
of course, their date's good looks—and by the 1920s this would include
the appearance of sexual awareness ("sex appeal" or "it")—ranked
high. Dating was a negotiation between boys and girls, but one in
which at least the physical component of girls' bargaining counters was
seen as both dangerous and perishable. Pretty girls, with more occasion to attract the most eligible boys and to hone their social skills,
married earlier and better. For those less favored by nature or less able
to attain the prescribed appearance, dating was a less pleasant process.[59] Boys, after all, initiated dates. And the double standard allowed
them a wider leeway in the kinds of pleasures they could seek from
the opposite sex and gave them the leeway of a later preferred marriage age.

Occasionally rebelling verbally against "girls who have dates four or
five out of the seven days of the week" and the "sort of contest" among
girls "to see who can get the most dates in one week," boys accepted
the new regime.[60] For them, it was something of a gain, in the sensual
pleasures of petting, in the tenderness of occasional intimate conversation, in the articulation of "popularity" with the bumptiously
democratic tone (and stratified structure) of the new, expanded, age-
homogenized high schools. "'It's just that I like to take her places,' explained one among the many suitors of Bette, the most popular date in
the junior class. 'You're sure to have a good time with her. She's never
a liability, you know that she'll be the belle of the ball. But really I'm
not crazy about her.'"[61]

The developing internal logic of the date can be discerned in the
statements of those whose dating experiences seemed to them imperfect enough that they wrote to newspaper advice columnists. In the

[59] Glen H. Elder, Jr., "Appearance and Education in Marriage Mobility," *American
Sociological Review* 34 (1969): 519–33; S. J. Holmes and C. E. Hatch, "Personal Ap-
pearance as Related to Scholastic Records and Marriage Selection in College Women,"
Human Biology 10 (1938): 65–76.

[60] Russ Brackett, letter in *Minneapolis West High News*, May 2, 1924; and "One of
the Many Sufferers," letter in *Little Falls The Comet's Tail*, February 11, 1930.

[61] Quoted in Caroline B. Zachry, *Emotion and Conduct in Adolescence* (New York:
Appleton-Century, 1940), p. 121. The study was conducted 1934–1939.

broad shifts in vocabulary, usage, and assumptions in these published letters can be seen the progressive definition of the institution of dating as it spread.[62] Urban readers were still only somewhat familiar with dating in 1920, and even the simplest rules of the dating system were not generally well known. Doris Blake's early correspondents often asked about when boys might be and should be invited to girls' homes (reflecting the transition from the older courtship tradition); but it was the goodnight kiss that provided the most common perplexity at this early date. W. A. wrote Blake: "I am a girl seventeen years of age. I have been going with a young man three years my senior, whom I love and admire very much. . . . Is 11 o'clock too late to arrive home from a show or some other place? Is it all right to allow him to kiss me good night, even though we are not engaged?" (August 7, 1920). Within a few years, kissing would imply almost no commitment. But in 1920, many youth were genuinely uncertain about the role of physical pleasure in the dating relationship.

The growing recognition that dates by design incorporated an ambiguous mixture of physical pleasure and self-restraint did not by itself remove all the perplexities of daters. They had still to learn how to

[62] I do not propose a naive reading of these letters, nor any kind of quantitative treatment. Internal evidence points to regular editing (even apart from selectivity) by the columnists, and scuttlebutt suggests some fabrication; newspaper readerships were narrower than the full range of the population, and only readers possessing both a sense of moderate anguish and a yen for publicity would even consider writing. On the other hand, if the letters did not smack of verisimilitude, the advice proffered would be read as a parody of itself; and to judge from the generally sober (while distinctly adolescent) tone of the great majority of the letters examined that dealt with problems in the early stages of boy-girl relationships, adolescent readers were in fact reached. (That parodies appeared frequently in the high school newspapers attests to the intense, if ambivalent, readership interest within this age group.)

For the assessment that follows, I read perhaps some 650 letters to two lovelorn columnists in three time periods—1920–21, 1925, and 1930–31—choosing and transcribing for closer analysis 326 of these, roughly divided among the three dates. Doris Blake was a syndicated columnist (first as "Doris Blake's Answers," later as "Doris Blake's Love Answers") in the *New York Daily News*, a pioneer tabloid appealing to relatively unsophisticated readers. Blake's column was the earliest I found that employed the letter-and-reply format (as contrasted with Dorothea Dix's essay-with-quotations format). Blake truncated her letters, obviously, especially by 1930, but by then I also had Martha Carr's evidently local and nonsyndicated "In My Opinion" column from the *St. Louis Post-Dispatch*, a newspaper of far higher tone, unfortunately. Although Carr regularized grammar and spelling, she allowed her correspondents to ramble on at considerable length, which was quite a boon for my purposes.

read the surface of the dating situation in a sophisticated fashion. R. S., for instance, couldn't fathom quite the implications of the behavior of the young man "that I care for." "He has declared his love for me also. But he goes to visit other girls and takes them to places and has never yet taken me anywhere. He's forever praising those girls. All this makes me doubt that he really cares for me. Do you think he does?" (December 27, 1920). R. S. simply does not know whether "caring for" is in any way articulated to the dating system, and, while she obviously perceives that there is such a thing as a "line," she lacks confidence in her ability to discern it in action.

The two 1920 correspondents just quoted presented their cases as individuals operating outside the peer context, and this is rather characteristic of the early letters. Dating, it would seem, early in its existence stranded relatively many people, who, uncomprehending, wrote to lovelorn columnists because they didn't know the rules. For whatever reason, their peer groups had seemingly failed to instruct them sufficiently. Shortly, however, a common complaint of the lovelorn was that their peers were all too much with them. Occasionally, the young women and men were troubled that other members of their peer group were in competition with them for the same dating partner, but more often they felt perplexed that for their partner the peer group's influence extended too far into the dating situation. Typically, the dating partner's inconstancy toward them was explained by such pressure. This was the case with "Heartbroken," a girl of sixteen, dating a boy of seventeen in 1925: "I love this fellow very much and I know he loves me. When we are at a party or at a dance he is always with me, and he always asks to take me home, and I let him. He is very nice, but when he is with a bunch of boys he just says hello and keeps right on going. I would like to know the reason for this (he is very bashful), because I love him. There are other boys whom I can go with, but I don't seem to take to any but him" (May 10, 1925). The use of "bashful" in this formulation is particularly instructive. "Heartbroken," more committed than her fellow to a unique emotional commitment, explains his responsiveness to his friends' groupishness as a social failing. Girls corporatively desired peer oversight of the dating system, but chided the limitations the clannishness of the boys imposed upon emotional commitment. (Sexual commitment, of course, was another matter again.)

Boys and girls did not agree entirely, but a rough peer consensus helped to define dating situations, to the considerable comfort of those involved. Symbol and gesture fitted into a changing youth code of dating that was nowhere written but was part of the oral tradition of youth, taught not by precept but in concrete cases. "I am 16, good looking and a good sport. A is 17, bashful, and not very good looking. His friends say he likes me" (Nellie K., April 29, 1925); "I am a young boy of 16 and am in love with a girl 5 months my junior. So far I have not told the girl anything but have confided in two of my boy friends. One of these boys went back and told her. As a result she was just a bit peeved" ("Troubled Nick," February 19, 1925).

Jealousy appeared increasingly often in the letters through this period, as the peer network—or, rather, the interlocking boy and girl peer networks—asserted a set of values and behaviors for dating. "I have known a boy for years and have been going with him for the last 14 months," wrote "Jealous" to Martha Carr in 1931. "I love him and I'm sure he likes me, but why on earth does he act so funny? He goes out with other girls and brings them where I can see them. He goes up to my friends' house [sic] and won't let them come down to my house. He takes one girl out and then asks her if she told me. I go out with others but I don't care for them. Tell me, is he just trying to make me jealous?" (October 5, 1931). Sexual jealousy, of course, may be a rather primal emotion, but in the case of the teenage lovelorn letters, it is not this kind of jealousy that crops up so often. Rather, jealousy was a sort of confused frustration, a product of divergent definitions of the two partners over the degree of articulation of the dating system with intimacy, on the one hand, and the peer popularity system, on the other. The publicness of the errant dating partner's behavior is striking in such letters: it is not failure in the inner resources of the heart that leads dating partners to write, but the inability to break free of the social snare in which they are enmeshed: "My friend's chum is keeping him away from me because my sister doesn't care to go out with him" ("Broken Hearted" to Blake, November 8, 1930).

Such shifts in the interpersonal dynamics of dating, as the institution evolved, did not fail to affect the emotional component of the institution and certainly not the way the emotions were conceptualized by those experiencing them. The reader of adolescent lovelorn letters from this period can hardly fail to observe the generally shallow connotation of the word "love." The notion, of course, was by 1920 carried into teenage courtship parlance through insipid romantic fiction of stage, screen, and print, so teenagers had good authority to feel love most transitorily. In the 1920 letters the vocabulary is limited to a few variant usages of "love," and occasional references to "care for." By 1925, the range of expression had widened a bit, with a new verb or two enlarging the capacity for discrimination, and a raft of new, conventionalized intensive adverbs suggesting a prescription not just to love, but to "love this girl dearly" (Luke to Blake, January 13, 1925).

Even such nonsense points to the capacity of the evolving dating system to instruct the emotions. By 1925, correspondents were being led to decide whether or not to assert a passionate relationship. "Troubled Sunny," in this vein, reasoned that "it must have been a case of love at first sight because as soon as I saw him I fell in love with him" (to Blake, May 14, 1925). The object of Sunny's affection said he felt the same way, but his continued talk of doings "with this blonde and that blonde" led Sunny to write Blake for help in defining the relationship. She explained, "He told me that the trouble with me is that I take things too seriously."

By 1930, even the brief letters to Blake indicate a concern for emotional precision. Connie wrote Blake (October 16, 1930) that her fellow "never told me he even cared for me." "Cared" is by now no synonym for love. "Doubtful" reported that her "fellow says he loves me. I like him as a friend" (to Blake, November 5, 1930). "Blue Peggy," seventeen years old, wrote that she felt left out because while "several of my girl friends have fellows and seem so in love," she herself "can't seem to get enthused" over her "several boy friends" (to Carr, September 17, 1931). In "Blue Peggy's" view, being "in love" was something one might be but at least should "seem" to be at seventeen, and that such a seeming might be approached through enthusiasm in dating, if only she could experience even that. In 1920, dating had to be subsumed to an emotional vocabulary developed under the romantic assumptions of "keeping company." By 1930, a considerably more modulated set of emotional responses was available, attuned to particular situations. One might even find uncensored cynicism, like that of the dialectically minded H. L., who had "found that the more a man spends on you [in dating], the more he likes you" (to Blake, October 31, 1930).

Dating took form. The letters mention an increasingly elaborate set of verbal categories and nonverbal symbols of dating affiliation—rings, pins, and peer-group insignia—and, even more significantly, of a more or less clearly differentiated set of dating stages. "Friend" and "fellow" were replaced by "boyfriend" and "girlfriend." The "keeping company" of the 1920 letters merged gradually into "going out." If "keeping company" still evoked the front porch, "going out" connoted going *out*, outside the immediate purview of watchful parents and outside assumptions regarding marriage as an explicit goal of the process. "Going out" implied one had somewhere to go.

In the 1930–1931 letters, "steady" relationships of one kind or another, including classic references to "going steady," virtually absent before, were quite common. Lacking such a defined stage, earlier daters like Tootsie had been confused: "I am a young girl of 17 and am really in love with a young man of 19. I have known him for over a year. We are not exactly engaged, but he has promised not to go with any other girls, nor I with any other boys. I am in a suburb now and am attending school. He goes to a university. I love this boy with all my heart. But some time it is such a temptation to go out with the boys" (May 25, 1925). A few years later, a metropolitan seventeen-year-old would have found no need to define her relationship with her young man residually. She would have known that going steady was easy to begin or terminate, combined clear behavioral prescriptions with undefined emotional commitment, and was only the boundary between casual dating and the steep and demanding road to marriage, not the first step on that road. Tootsie could have negotiated with her young man for gradually enhanced emotional intimacy without such risk of irrevocable sexual intimacy or premature marriage, possible in an overheated, unstable relationship of "not exactly" engagement.

IV

Boys' commitment to symmetrical affectionate relationships was no doubt limited, but a limited commitment was all that was needed to establish the particular rhythm of the dating system. Once in place, fueled in no small part by the sexual energies it brought into play, the dating system itself was consequential, a mechanism for a gradual shift in normative categories. One sixteen-year-old boy, for instance, was just barely able to retain the strongly engrained good girl–bad girl distinction: "The girls I know can be divided into two classes—passionate but dumb and frigid but intelligent. . . . I believe my desire for love is quite proper in view of the fact that it embodies no sexual relations. I really despise my friends who speak of all girls in terms of their flesh. Yet it seems impossible to find a girl who is both intelligent and human."[63]

The date, as a bargain, was unromantic even if affectionate. In dating, style mattered a great deal: performance was on the whole more important than the unmediated expression of feelings. Whereas both "crushes" and love affairs had been seen to be full of "idealization," the very ordinariness of dating placed practical limits upon the amount of romantic idealization that courtship could now support.[64] The success of the dating system encouraged a set of rules, rules of performance more than of feeling, rules that even young boys and girls could learn. Thus, Ernie, thirteen, stoutly denied in 1931 that "I want to call on girls and take them out," but admitted to having girlfriends and that in defiance of his parents' wishes he liked "to have friendly talks with girls over the telephone." "Every boy my age likes to have money to spend and to dress up," Ernie lectured Martha Carr (April 3, 1931).

Thus propelled, the whole schedule of dating was accelerated, especially as the prosperity of the post–World War II period permitted younger boys to gain access to the money a proper date required[65] and no doubt to learn to enjoy (with the help of peer-group games) the controlled but overt sexuality that was a part of dating. By the postwar period, adolescents' parents as often as not had themselves dated. Most ordinarily, of course, normatively—and interpersonally—structured restraint outweighed sexual desire, but there can be little question that the success of the dating system placed a downward pressure

---

[63] Quoted in Zachry, *Emotion and Conduct*, pp. 389–90.

[64] Waller's commitment to a conception of love in which idealization played a large part, I believe, blinded him to the affectionate element in dating and led him to believe that dating and courtship were wholly different activities. See Waller, "Rating and Dating"; Waller, *The Family*, chap. 8. See also Clifford Kirkpatrick and Theodore Caplow, "Courtship in a Group of Minnesota Students," *American Journal of Sociology* 51 (1945): 114–25.

[65] University of Michigan, Survey Research Center, "Adolescent Girls," mimeographed (n.p., n.d. [1956 or 1957], p. 134; John C. Flanagan et al., *The American High School Student* (Cooperative Research Project No. 635, multilith (Pittsburgh: University of Pittsburgh Project Talent Office, 1964), appendix tabulations of Q. 51.

on the age of marriage. The ideas about marital timing that had evolved among daters in the early decades of that institution's existence were realized after World War II.[66] Thereafter, material circumstances permitted a simultaneous lowering of the marriage age and a considerable prolongation of schooling, thus bringing dating and marriage into closer articulation.

For girls in particular these developments had alarming implications. When dating and marriage became closely linked in time, "popularity" became even more prescriptive for girls, and its attainment precluded for them ambitions that looked much beyond the confines of the peer group. Students understood this well: "To get dates you must be liked by the kids and to be liked you must take part in the activities around school. If you keep your nose in the book all of the time and don't show any interest in the other kids, you are not even considered as a prospect for dating."[67] Quantitative confirmation of the immediate impact of this orientation upon girls' lives is a major theme of James S. Coleman's classic *The Adolescent Society*, based on late-1950s data from high school students.[68] A researcher who reinterviewed these respondents in the mid-1970s found that high school dating frequency was one of very few prior variables that had a continuing impact upon women's adult lives, although it had but little upon men's. Popular girls had had relatively little educational ambition and had attained relatively little in the educational system. Instead, they had married young.[69] The dating system had permitted them considerable freedom of choice, but the end product of their choice was nevertheless sharply constrained by the asymmetries of contemporaneous marital roles. Thus constrained, women sought fulfillment in their children.[70]

[66] John Modell, "Normative Aspects of American Marriage Timing since World War II," *Journal of Family History* 5 (1980): 210–34.

[67] Quoted in John Richard Crist, "High School Dating as a Behavior System" (Ph.D. dissertation, University of Missouri, 1951), p. 153.

[68] James S. Coleman, *The Adolescent Society* (New York: The Free Press of Glencoe, 1961).

[69] Margaret Mooney Marini, "The Transition to Adulthood: Sex Differences in Educational Attainment and Age at Marriage," *American Sociological Review* 43 (1978): 498, 501.

[70] This argument is based on intensive analysis of the textual materials in the more than one hundred questionnaires gathered from eighteen- and nineteen-year-old single women in 1955 as part of the first Growth of American Families Study. Alice Robbin of

Beginning with the wartime and continuing until the late 1950s marriage was followed by first childbirth more and more quickly and uniformly, as dating led more directly and uniformly to marriage and for women to a life substantially within the confines of that institution. For young men, as one would expect, early marriage was neither so closely related to dating career nor so consequential. [71]

This pattern did not hold. Women's age at first marriage rose in the 1960s; first childbirth became progressively postponed after marriage; and total fertility declined sharply. [72] Already by the 1960s, youth began dating later than they had a decade before. The term still exists, but it is far indeed from capturing as once it did what boys and girls do together. [73]

the University of Wisconsin Program and Data Library has been most generous with her time in helping me gain access to these documents.

[71] Alan E. Bayer, "Early Dating and Early Marriage," *Journal of Marriage and the Family* 30 (1968): 632; Paul Ronald Voss, "Social Determinants of Age at First Marriage in the United States" (Ph.D. dissertation, University of Michigan, 1975), pp. 239–48.

[72] The best demographic account of this trend is in Amy Ong Tsui, "A Study of the Family Formation Process among U.S. Marriage Cohorts" (Ph.D. dissertation, University of Chicago, 1978), especially pp. 92, 102, 160. A discussion of the voluntary aspects of this demographic change is found in John Modell, Frank F. Furstenberg, Jr., and Douglas Strong, "The Timing of Marriage in the Transition to Adulthood: Continuity and Change, 1860–1975," in *Turning Points*, ed. John Demos and Sarane S. Boocock (Supplement to *American Journal of Sociology* 84 [1978]: S138–42). For the impact of early marriage on women, see Larry Lee Bumpass, "Age at Marriage as a Variable in Socioeconomic Differentials in Fertility" (Ph.D. dissertation, University of Michigan, 1968), pp. 149–50.

[73] James V. Scanlon, *Self-reported Health Behavior and Attitudes of Youths 12–17 Years*, Vital and Health Statistics, Series 11, No. 147, (Washington, D.C.: U.S. Department of Health, Education and Welfare, 1975), p. 73; Robert C. Sorensen, *Adolescent Sexuality in Contemporary America* (New York: World Publishing, 1973), pp. 108–15; Melvin Zelnik, John F. Kantner, and Kathleen Ford, *Sex and Pregnancy in Adolescence*, Sage Library of Social Research, Vol. 133, (Beverly Hills, Calif.: Sage Publications, 1981), p. 44.

ELIZABETH PLECK

The Whipping Post for Wife Beaters, 1876–1906

"Wifebeating," wrote one eminent nineteenth-century American lawyer, "is a crime of brute force where the strong beat the weak with blows."[1] Many Americans in that period believed that the worst of men were brutes by nature, unable to control their animal impulses. Building more prisons to house the drunkard, the tramp, and the abuser of women and children had failed to deter such men from committing crimes. Other forms of punishment, therefore, were required for the protection of pure women from the beast in man and for the protection of the public from the criminal class. Eminently respectable lawyers, judges, and other law enforcement officials led a campaign to punish wife beaters with the whipping post. Between 1876 and 1906 bills to punish wife beaters with the whipping post were introduced in twelve states and the District of Columbia.[2] Judges of criminal courts, presidents of police boards, district attorneys, and grand juries supported this punishment. Editorials in major newspapers from the *Chicago Herald* to the *Washington Post* championed the whipping post. Even the national association of the Congregational church was in favor. Nonetheless, the opponents of the whipping post far outnumbered its supporters. Whipping post bills were resoundingly defeated, except in three states. The campaign never gained momentum, and its three victories came, almost by chance, in Maryland in 1882, Delaware in 1901, and Oregon in 1905.

It is surprising to learn of a campaign that not only regarded wife

[1] Clark Bell, "Wife Beaters and Their Punishments," *Medico-Legal Journal* 20 (1902–1903): 579.
[2] The twelve states that considered legislation to punish wife beating with the whipping post were California (1876), Missouri (1879), Maryland (1882), Massachusetts (1884 and 1905), Pennsylvania (1885), New Hampshire (1885), New York (1895), Virginia (1899–1900), Illinois (1899), New Jersey (1899, 1901), Delaware (1901), and Oregon (1905). It was also considered by the U.S. Congress, acting as the legislative body for the District of Columbia, in 1906.

beating as a crime, but one serious enough to warrant flogging a man. Far back in English common law, the husband possessed the right to administer moderate correction to his wife. It is true that a few U.S. state appellate court judges upheld this rule, but even these men considered correction that went beyond the moderate assault and battery. Moreover, the vast majority of American states held that the common law rule of moderate correction had never been law in the United States. The Virginia state legislature even refused to repeal the old common law rule for fear of giving the impression that wife beating had ever enjoyed legal sanction. By about 1900, eleven states had passed laws punishing wife beating as a misdemeanor, and most of those states without specific statutes against wife beating still regarded it as assault and battery.[3]

The idea of whipping the wife beater originated in England during the period of public concern about armed robbery and was supported by the apparent belief that a man who assaulted his wife would also beat his neighbor or a stranger. British magistrate Thomas Phinn first introduced in Parliament a bill to flog wife beaters in 1854. It was defeated, but supporters of the bill made four more attempts to gain its passage, each without success. Nonetheless, the idea of whipping criminals found favor in England. Parliament passed in 1863 a law punishing armed robbers with flogging and another in 1876 providing for the whipping of juvenile delinquents.[4] American supporters of the whipping post often referred to the success of English flogging legislation in virtually eliminating the crime of armed robbery. New York City adopted a similar act, and Virginia, influenced by English law, passed a law to punish youthful criminals with whipping. There were also a few domestic precedents for whipping as a punishment, which had been a common punishment in the colonies. Delaware had retained its whipping post as a punishment for a variety of crimes, although wife beating was not one of them, and the territory of New

---

[3]Irving Browne, "Wife Beating and Imprisonment," *American Law Review* 25 (July–August, 1891): 551–69; Elizabeth Pleck, "Wife Beating in Nineteenth Century America," *Victimology* 4, no. 1 (1979): 60–74.

[4]Margaret May, "Violence in the Family: An Historical Perspective," in *Violence and the Family*, ed. J. P. Martin (Chichester, England: John Wiley and Sons, 1978), pp. 144–45.

Mexico, which could not afford to build a jail, punished mule stealing with whipping.[5]

The first bill to punish wife beating with the whipping post in the United States was introduced in California in 1876. It was defeated, and little is known about its sponsors or its opponents.[6] Three years later the Missouri legislature considered a bill to punish with flogging petty larceny, wife beating, and cruelty to children. One Missouri legislator believed it would save the state the cost of imprisoning wife beaters. An opponent, without elaborating, argued just the opposite. Another legislator claimed that to whip a man was to destroy his manhood. These men apparently carried the day, since the bill was handily defeated.[7]

Maryland in 1882 became the first state to pass a bill punishing brutal wife beating with the whipping post. The law provided a whipping of not more than forty lashes, a one-year term in prison, or both a whipping and a prison term. The whipping was to be administered by a sheriff within the walls of the county jail. The sponsor of the bill was a prominent lawyer and member of the American Bar Association. He pointed out that Maryland's neighboring state Delaware still used the whipping post to punish many crimes, and he made an impassioned plea on behalf of the wives who suffered beatings on Saturday nights from drunken husbands: whipping was an appropriate punishment for such cruelty because it "did not make the poor woman suffer as well."[8] Although opponents believed whipping to be a cruel and barbarous punishment, they were in the minority, and the bill passed by a margin of two to one.[9] Because of the legislative success in Maryland, similar bills were introduced in the next few years in Massachusetts, Pennsylvania, and New Hampshire. But opposition from the leadership of

[5] "Cruel and Unusual Punishment," *Iowa Law Review* 12, no. 1 (December, 1926): 88–89.

[6] *Woman's Journal*, January 29, 1876.

[7] *Appleton's Annual Cyclopaedia and Register of Important Events*, 1879, s.v. "Missouri," p. 639.

[8] *Report of the Tenth Annual Meeting of the American Bar Association* (Philadelphia: T. and J. W. Johnson, 1887), p. 64.

[9] Maryland, House of Delegates, *Journal of the Proceedings of the House of Delegates of Maryland, General Assembly, January Session 1882*, pp. 62, 199, 253, 448. The Maryland act only punished husbands who brutally beat their wives. Many husbands pleaded guilty to a lesser charge and thus escaped the whipping post.

both political parties and from religious groups led to the resounding defeat of these bills.

Although most of the attempts to pass this legislation failed, the campaign nonetheless attracted the interest of highly respected and wealthy lawyers and judges, most of whom were Republicans. It had three preeminent leaders. One was Clark Bell, a lawyer who made his fortune as an attorney for the Union Pacific Railroad. Considered an expert in medical law, Bell helped increase the legal role of psychiatrists, often needed to testify about the sanity of the defendant, and expand the functions of the coroner. Bell was elected a member of the Medico-Legal Society of New York and soon became its president. In 1884 he began the society's journal and became its editor. He reprinted in the journal his extensive correspondence with judges, lawyers, and police chiefs, most of whom favored the whipping post. He also sponsored forums to debate the efficacy of the whipping post, which he came to favor for juvenile delinquents as well as wife beaters. Although his cause was unpopular, he persisted in it for almost three decades.

A second leader of the campaign was Simeon Baldwin. Born in New Haven, Connecticut, in 1840, Baldwin was a graduate of Yale. He studied law in his father's law office, at Yale, and at Harvard and was a faculty member of the Yale Law School from the time he joined it in 1869 until 1919. He was also a judge in the state supreme court and eventually became its chief justice. Baldwin was elected governor of Connecticut for two terms, and his only electoral defeat came in his bid to become the state's U.S. senator. One of the most widely respected lawyers of his day, he was credited with the growth of professional legal study at Yale. He became president of many of the organizations he joined, such as the International Law Association, the American Social Science Association, the Association of American Law Schools, the American Historical Association, the American Political Science Association, and the American Bar Association. Baldwin was first introduced to the idea of the whipping post in 1885. That year Daniel Chamberlain, a New York lawyer, prominent Republican, and former governor of South Carolina during Reconstruction, presented a resolution to the American Bar Association calling for a study of the desirability of whipping as a punishment. Baldwin was a member of the association's study committee. His committee recommended the whipping post resolution, although the membership of the association later voted it down by a large margin. He continued his advocacy of the whipping post in an article in the *Yale Law Journal* in 1899 in which he also favored castration as a punishment for rape. Two years later he renewed his plea for whipping wife beaters and juvenile delinquents, but he dropped his demand for the castration of rapists. As late as 1913, Baldwin was still speaking in favor of the whipping post. Although he was considered the "first citizen of Connecticut" and a great lawyer and jurist, Baldwin was regarded as a fanatic on this issue.

A third major leader of this campaign was Robert Adams. He first introduced a whipping post bill when he represented Philadelphia in the Pennsylvania State Senate. Adams was born into a wealthy Philadelphia family that traced its ancestry back to the Revolution. After serving a brief term as ambassador to Brazil, he was elected from Philadelphia's silk-stocking district to the U.S. House of Representatives, where he served six terms. He helped draft the declaration of war against Spain in 1898. In 1906, Adams dusted off the bill he had introduced in Pennsylvania some nineteen years before and introduced it into the House of Representatives. He read into the *Congressional Record* the same report he had written two decades before, without mentioning what year the statistics were compiled. His colleagues challenged him, and after scoring this initial victory, they went on to chide Adams as a bachelor who knew nothing of the circumstances that led men to beat their wives. Four months later Adams, alone in his hotel suite, put a pistol to his mouth and pulled the trigger. He left a note saying that he was deeply in debt; and rumors circulated that he had been dying of cancer.[10]

Although these three leaders kept their campaign alive for several decades, they cannot be credited with any of its legislative victories. But because of their prestige and influence, they were able to speak on this subject before the Social Science Association, the American Association of Physicians and Surgeons, and the Connecticut Board for Charities and Corrections. Their influence was probably the main reason that whipping post bills were introduced in eight states along the Eastern seaboard, although they were unable to carry their campaign to legislatures in the deep South, the Midwest, or the West.

[10] *Philadelphia Inquirer*, February 2, 1906.

The campaign also interested Elbridge Gerry and John Shortall. Gerry was a founder of the New York Society to Protect Children from Cruelty, an organization designed to punish parents who cruelly beat their children. Yet Gerry was quoted as saying that "a good sound licking is the only thing" that would do a criminal any good.[11] Shortall, the founder of the Illinois Humane Society, had beliefs just as paradoxical. Punishing juvenile crime with flogging, he told legislators, belonged as part of the movement to "save the child."[12] Notably absent from this campaign were any victims of wife beating. But their absence, claimed the proponents, only served to underscore the necessity for the campaign. These women were so "bound and beaten" that they could not cry out, and although "their sighs are secret, their tears unseen, . . . they are a river, a current like the Amazon of uncontrollable anguish."[13]

Most of the opponents of this legislation were state legislators who considered whipping barbarous. In New Jersey church groups opposed it. Vigorous opposition to the whipping post bill when introduced in Pennsylvania came from the Philadelphia Society for Alleviating the Miseries of Public Prisons, a largely Quaker group of prison reformers. For decades Delaware Quakers opposed the state's whipping post and pillory.

Suffragist opinion was about equally divided about whether to punish wife beaters with the whipping post. Reverend Phebe Hanaford, an ordained Congregationalist minister and a founding member of the first woman's club in the United States, favored the whipping post as the only means of ensuring the protection of women. The most prominent suffragist supporter of the whipping post was Lucy Stone, the leader of the American Woman's Suffrage Association and a longtime advocate of women's rights. She believed that every state should erect a whipping post because criminal penalties had not deterred wife beaters. Only the dread of pain and the disgrace of being beaten would eliminate wife beating.[14] On the other hand, her husband, Henry

[11] Howard Jenkins, "Live Wood in Our Whipping Post," *Lippincott's Magazine* 23, no. 135 (March, 1899): 368.

[12] Illinois Humane Society, *Thirtieth Annual Report* (Chicago: Privately printed, 1899), pp. 56–58.

[13] Clark Bell, "The Cat as a Deterrent for Crime," *Journal of the American Institute of Criminal Law and Criminology* 8 (May, 1912–March, 1913): 946.

[14] *Woman's Journal*, July 11, 1885; *Woman's Journal*, January 29, 1876.

Blackwell, was opposed to whipping wife beaters and believed that woman's suffrage was the only long-term solution to the problem. Men would treat women better when they learned that the law considered women the equals of men. A female electorate, Blackwell believed, would demand enforcement of criminal laws against wife beating. Blackwell's sister-in-law, Antoinette Brown Blackwell, also opposed the whipping post. She was one of the first female graduates of Oberlin College and the first woman to be ordained a minister of a recognized denomination in the United States. Believing the whipping post to be a perversion of Christianity, she insisted that there was "some kindred feeling at the bottom of the heart of the worst and basest child of the Common Father."[15] Even a dedicated anticlericalist like Matilda Gage was opposed to the whipping post for wife beaters. Gage was a past president of the National American Woman's Suffrage Association and one of the authors of the multivolume *History of Woman Suffrage*. She insisted that the "remedy for crimes against women" did "not lie in the punishment of offenders, but in different sentiments in regard to woman in both church and state."[16] These opinions were heard only as backstage voices, and none of these suffragists ever participated in any legislative campaign. Nonetheless, Bell and the other leaders of the campaign for the whipping post favored women's suffrage, but they preferred to emphasize the suffering of innocent women rather than the inequality between the sexes. They believed women received equal treatment not so much from the civil as the criminal law. They regarded the whipping post as a symbol for a civilization that treated women equally, unlike "barbarous nations" which "treated their women as inferiors."[17]

The importance and the appeal of the whipping post can be found in general features of Anglo-American culture, particularly in those that surfaced during the last quarter of the nineteenth century. This culture espoused a belief in the sanctity of the home as a refuge from the world. This belief divided the world into the male sphere of politics and business, and the female sphere of the home, where the

[15] Antoinette Brown Blackwell, "Corporal Punishment for Crime," *Medico-Legal Journal* 17, no. 1 (1899): 113.

[16] Matilda Joslyn Gage, *Woman, Church and State* (Watertown, Mass.: Persephone Press, 1981), p. 145.

[17] "Wife Beaters and Their Punishment," *Medico-Legal Journal* 21 (1903–1904): 316.

woman presided, offering love to her children and comfort to her husband. In the marriage ceremony the husband had promised to honor and cherish his wife, but in beating his wife he broke his wedding vows and defiled the sanctity of the home. Women were weak, innocent, and helpless—they were unable to defend themselves against a brutish man. The proponents of the whipping post funished examples of maimed, bruised, and bleeding wives, most of whom were mothers, women who had been knocked senseless on the floor, kicked in the face, or beaten while struggling "to protect the innocent babe in her arms."[18] Rhetoric about "the sobs, the moans, the tears of wretched victims" made for a highly emotional appeal. The wife was invariably virtuous and innocent; her husband was a disgrace to his sex, a monster, a brute, or at least a beast driven mad by alcohol. Some of the whipping post bills were designed to protect women or women and children. Elbridge Gerry of the New York Society to Protect Children from Cruelty wanted the law in New York to flog child molestors and fathers guilty of incest. The whipping post bill introduced in Massachusetts would have lashed any male who "beats, bruises, or mutilates" his wife or any other female.[19]

It might appear that the desire to protect women and children grew out of male chivalry, rather than any impulse belonging only to the late Victorian period. But the chivalric ideal, which enjoyed a resurgence in the poetry of Tennyson and in the beliefs of Victorians, was joined with a more active view of the state, in which women's temperance organizations, societies to protect children from cruelty, social purity organizations, and many women's clubs and suffrage organizations marched forward under the banner of protecting helpless women and children. It was insufficient for the state to control the public activity of (lower-class) men; it also had to police the private sphere—the family. Regardless of whether the campaign was led by women or men, these movements shared a view that the state, through the criminal law, had to protect women and children even if invading the privacy of the family was required and that pure and innocent children were in great peril from bestial man.

A second reason for the interest in this issue was a desire to reacti-

<hr/>

[18] Ibid., p. 312.
[19] "Wife Beating and the Lash," *Medico-Legal Journal* 22 (1904–1905): p. 522. The bill proposed in Massachusetts applied only to husbands who assaulted their wives with a dangerous weapon.

vate the criminal law in punishing sin, as the Puritans once so actively had done. Because a literal interpretation of the Bible was back in vogue, it was more acceptable to justify whipping with reference to Exodus or Deuteronomy. Although the United States was a Christian nation, the law did not reflect Christian concerns until moral vigilantes, beginning in the 1870s, began to influence state and national law. The Comstock law prohibited the dissemination of immoral literature through the mail. Liberal divorce statutes were eliminated and antiabortion laws were passed. Women began to crusade against the evil of alcohol. Christian reformers agitated for a constitutional amendment recognizing Christianity and won state and local laws enforcing Sunday closings. Abortion, intemperance, and sexual immorality were private sins deserving of criminal legislation, along with gambling, violations of the Sabbath, and use of tobacco or drugs. The public was concerned, as Morton Keller points out, because of the "persistence of religious morality, combined with the special tensions and anxieties that came with industrialism."[20] United States criminal law rested heavily on the assumption that private acts had public consequences, and there was a natural impetus to increase the areas of conduct subject to penal sanctions. Wife beating could easily fit with this catalog of private acts to be considered immoral and criminal, especially inasmuch as the wife beater was often a sinful drunkard. It was easy to sandwich wife beaters among the sinners and ne'er-do-wells. A Nebraska statute, passed in 1901, permitted cities to punish abusers of their families, along with vagrants, tramps, beggars, prostitutes, pickpockets, gamblers, burglars, thieves, ball-game players, swindlers, and suspicious persons.[21]

There was another less frequent but nonetheless persistent concern behind this campaign—the issue of race. In the South, most of the men arrested or convicted of wife beating were black. After Maryland erected its whipping post, in 1882 the first husband to be flogged was black. In Delaware, between 1901 and 1942, six whites and fifteen blacks were flogged for wife beating and also two whites and five blacks were flogged for the crime of assault to ravish.[22] In a state where in

<hr />

[20] Morton Keller, *Affairs of State: Public Life in Late Nineteenth Century America* (Cambridge, Mass.: Belknap Press, 1977), p. 807.

[21] Nebraska, *Revised Statutes*, p. 101.

[22] Robert Caldwell, *Red Hannah: Delaware's Whipping Post* (Philadelphia: University of Pennsylvania Press, 1947), p. 129.

1940 blacks were only 13 percent of the population, two-thirds of those flogged for rape and wife beating were black. Even in states without a whipping post, husbands punished for assaulting their wives were often black. For instance, most of the men arrested for wife beating in the District of Columbia around the turn of the century were black.[23] The South Carolina State Constitutional Convention, meeting in 1895, found a way to make use of these facts in helping to disenfranchise the state's still considerable black electorate. They amended the state's constitution to deny the franchise to men convicted of housebreaking, receiving stolen goods, breach of trust with fraudulent intention, fornication, sodomy, assault with intent to ravish, miscegenation, incest, larceny, and wife beating.[24] At first glance, it is surprising that the issue of wife beating would have appealed to white Southerners, since they believed the problem to be one largely found among blacks, where the victim was a black woman. (It differed from rape, where alleged motivation was the protection of white women). Southern legislators resolved this problem by avoiding the rhetorical flourishes that Northerners used in describing the sufferings of the woman and emphasizing instead the need to control the vicious impulses of the black man. At the end of Reconstruction, Southern white legislators found this issue an additional means for controlling the black criminal and the black voter.

They believed the whipping post especially suited for black criminals, who possessed innate criminal tendencies and whose inferior culture exhibited no respect for law and order. Black criminals actually enjoyed imprisonment because they could lie idle there, eat free meals, and associate on the basis of equality with whites. Imprisonment was not a disgrace for the black criminal; after release, he quickly rejoined his underworld comrades. But blacks especially feared a whipping, because they associated it with slavery. Still, advocates of the whipping post often remarked that in Delaware no white man was ever whipped twice, implying that whipping of blacks would have to be

[23] U.S., Congress, E. D. Morrell, *Report from the Committee on the District of Columbia on H. 8133, for Infliction of Corporal Punishment upon Persons Beating Their Wives*, 59th Cong., 1st sess., vol. 1, 1906, H. Rept. 1057, p. 4906.

[24] *Constitution of the State of South Carolina, Ratified in Convention, December 4, 1895* (Abbeville, S.C.: Hugh Wilson, 1900), pp. 10–11. See also David Duncan Wallace, *The South Carolina Constitution of 1895* (Columbia, S.C.: Bureau of Publications, 1927), pp. 30–38.

repeated because their criminal tendencies outweighed their fear of whipping. Statements like these were uttered by Northerners as well as Southerners, but they surfaced more frequently in the debates about the whipping post by the Southern legislatures, where they were used to make a more effective although ultimately unsuccessful appeal.[25]

The campaign to reintroduce the whipping post also coincided with a resurgence of mob violence, of vigilantes in the West, lynch mobs in the South, and White Caps in the Middle West. Both a whipping and a lynching were simple, certain, severe, and painful punishments of convicted or alleged criminals. The whipping, however, was a sentence imposed by the courts and administered by a sheriff, but a lynching was a mob action, in which the alleged offender was punished by the community, rather than by an agent of the state. The criminal survived a whipping, but there was no survival from a lynching. Both campaigns grew out of moral fervor and a desire to reintroduce harsher punishments against criminals. They even shared a common concern about wife beating. There were a few instances in southern and western states where husbands who brutally beat or murdered their wives were lynched.[26] But the advocates of the whipping post opposed lynching. They believed that if the criminal law were more punitive, citizens would not resort to extralegal mob action. Nonetheless, it would be a mistake to overemphasize the racial overtones and vigilantism in this campaign.[27] After all, the idea began in England and appealed in a

[25] Simeon Baldwin, *The American Judiciary* (New York: The Century, 1905), p. 246; idem, "Whipping as a Mode of Punishment," *Journal of the American Institute of Criminal Law and Criminology* 2 (May, 1911–March, 1912): 341–343.

[26] Gage, *Woman, Church and State*, p. 331; National Association for the Advancement of Colored People, *Thirty Years of Lynching in the United States, 1889–1918* (New York: National Association for the Advancement of Colored People, 1919), pp. 63, 80, 82, 92.

[27] Richard Maxwell Brown, in *Strain of Violence: Historical Studies of American Violence and Vigilantism* (New York: Oxford University Press, 1975), p. 177, argues that Simeon Baldwin favored the whipping post and castration because of "the prevalence of lynch law and vigilantism in the nineteenth century [which] had brutalized attitudes." However, he neglects to point out that these attitudes were just as prevalent in England, where lynch law was unknown. He also conveys his attitude toward wife beating: "The White Caps were using whipping all over the country as an extra legal punishment for wifebeating, immorality, shiftlessness, and petty thievery—precisely the sort of *small offense* [italics added] against which the movement to legalize whipping was mainly directed."

country where there was no lynching and only a few blacks. Mob violence and racism were useful, but not absolutely necessary reasons for favoring the whipping post. Northerners and Westerners feared drunkards or tramps, immigrants or juvenile delinquents. Everywhere the designated criminal was of the lowest caste, a brute whose animal impulses could not be controlled by conventional punishments.

The issue of wife beating combined the need to protect women and children from brutish men with a more general anxiety about the formation of a class of dangerous criminals. The arrival of the immigrant, episodes of severe unemployment, and the growth of foul-smelling, dirty industrial cities provoked fears that crime had become a permanent feature of American society. The ranks of the criminal class continued to grow, while the weapons at the disposal of society were reduced in number and efficiency. Sentimental and confused reformers, it was believed, were more concerned about the condition of the criminal than about the suffering of his victim. Too often it was impossible to secure a conviction for notorious offenders. Nonetheless, there were so many criminals that at least some of them were convicted, thus swelling the prison population. For the hardened criminal (as well as for blacks), fear of imprisonment did not deter crime. Prisons had actually helped to perpetuate crime by confining men to a foul and contaminating atmosphere.

Public attitudes had not always been so conservative. Just after the Civil War, several Southern states had adopted new constitutions forbidding corporal punishments of criminals. The *New York Times* in that era had challenged Delaware's whipping post, which it considered incompatible with "the precepts of decency, civilization, and Christianity."[28] Several states had abolished capital punishment. Influential reformers even claimed that crime rose because of the poverty in which the criminal had been raised. Then the wave of reform subsided, and toward the end of the century some of the reformers began to wonder if the pendulum had not swung too far in the wrong direction. In the midst of a major depression, the public came to fear the tramp begging at the back door. States that had abolished the death penalty now reintroduced it. Stiffer criminal penalties were called for,

[28] *Wilmington Daily Commercial*, April 13, 1867, p. 2, quoted in Caldwell, *Red Hannah*, p. 19.

and lawyers demanded police surveillance of former offenders convicted more than once.[29] Some proposed that felons should be permanently disenfranchised.

The public was concerned about violent crime, especially when the victim was "innocent and defenseless." Baldwin's committee of the American Bar Association favored whipping as a punishment for wife beating, "or assaults committed with slung shots, sand bags, brass knuckles, or similar weapons."[30] Shortall of the Illinois Humane Society was concerned about violent crimes, especially those perpetrated by youth. In the bill he introduced in the Illinois state legislature, he hoped to punish wife beating, armed robbery, child molestation, and habitual criminals.

Because of the fear of a crime wave, the most frequent argument, and the one with the most appeal, was that the whipping post would deter wife beating. A punishment had to be as serious as the crime it was designed to punish, and it had to make an impression on the criminal as well as convey to the potential criminal the seriousness with which violation of the law would be regarded. A fine was not serious or severe enough punishment for wife beating, and it imposed financial suffering on the victim herself. Imprisonment had not worked, either. Criminals did not think about the amount of time they would have to spend in prison: they were incapable of distinguishing between a sentence of a few months and one of many years. Because they were lacking in moral sentiments, they did not suffer any disgrace from having been sent to prison.

Proponents of the whipping post believed that the power of love kept most men honest and law-abiding, but the brutes and monsters who formed the dangerous criminal classes could only be controlled by fear, pain, or disgrace. The great value of a whipping was that it combined all three. The one thing that the wife beater feared was pain. Once he had been whipped, he would be so afraid of receiving another whipping that he would cease to beat his wife. Pain was also a highly appropriate punishment because it inflicted physical suffering on one who had caused it, meeting force with force, blow with blow. Reverend Phebe Hanaford believed that the whipping post would deter the

[29] American Bar Association, *Report of the Ninth Annual Meeting of the American Bar Association* (Philadelphia: Dando Printing and Publishing, 1886), p. 287.
[30] Ibid., pp. 286–93.

wife beater from repeating his violence, for he "learns two lessons: one, how it feels to be beaten, and the other, that the law will not allow him to whip his wife without inflicting the same upon himself."[31] Although the proponents of the whipping post claimed they were interested only in deterrence, not retribution, their statements suggested otherwise. The chief justice of the Delaware Supreme Court would have liked to have "the wife whip [her husband] if I could get her to do so, and [I] would like to stand beside her at the time."[32] Justice Lore's remarks were only slightly more graphic than those of the typical proponent of the whipping post, and others described the bleeding back of a man crying out in pain from the sting of the lash. Some of the whipping post bills even prescribed that the lash should be laid on a bare back. In keeping with this attitude, a Boston judge, widely quoted in out-of-state papers, longed for "the day when I can order the lash to be applied to the naked back of the man who assaults his wife."[33] Most of the proponents had in mind the use of the cat-o-nine-tails as the instrument of punishment. It consisted of nine leather cords, each about an inch wide and two feet long, attached to a stick about a foot and a half long.

Once the wife beater felt pain, it was assumed, he would desist from beating his family. (This argument seems somewhat muddled, since the wife beater probably had encountered violence at the hands of his own father or at least in a fistfight.) Inflicting pain on the wife beater, as the proponents suggested, represented a rejection of Victorian attitudes toward pain. Antivivisectionists were concerned that animals not suffer pain, and doctors were provided drugs to spare their patients from experiencing pain. These lawyers and judges opposed this sentimental attitude, which they believed was simply an additional manifestation of false humanitarianism and vitiated moral fiber. Others claimed that a whipping deterred because it caused disgrace, rather than pain. Flogging made the wife beater feel so ashamed of himself that he repented for his misdeed. Even if he failed to repent, he was at least disgraced in the eyes of his comrades, who would no longer associate with him. Shunned by them, he would be forced to

---

[31] The Rev. Phebe A. Hanaford, "The Whipping Post for Wife Beaters," *Medico-Legal Journal* 17, no. 1 (1899): 109.

[32] Quoted in Caldwell, *Red Hannah*, p. 33.

[33] Quoted in Caldwell, *Red Hannah*, p. 33.

seek the companionship of honest men. But if flogging caused disgrace, why not branding, perhaps with the letters *W. B.*, as the *New
York World* seriously suggested? Here the proponents drew the line.
They were opposed to branding because it caused permanent disgrace
and made it impossible for the criminal to repent.

The whipping post for wife beaters, the proponents claimed, had
been a great success. Flogging had been a valuable means of discipline
in the English army, and its adoption had put an end to armed robbery,
once prevalent in London. In Maryland the crime of wife beating had
been virtually eliminated. The publicity in the case of a wife beater
who was sentenced to a year in jail and twenty lashes, it was said,
served to deter others, leading to a reduction in the number of arrests
for wife beating from 131 in 1884 to 67 in 1885. By the following year,
the number of wife-beating cases was cut in half, and the police believed that the cases they were receiving were less serious ones.[34] Decades later, it was alleged that after only three convictions, the crime of
wife beating had been eliminated in Oregon.[35] These extravagant
claims were perhaps necessary to overcome objections to the whipping
post. If it could be shown that only a few whippings would be required,
then those who were squeamish about harsh punishments might be
won over. Even though Delaware did not punish wife beating with the
whipping post until 1901, it became the most frequent example of the
efficacy of whipping as a punishment. It was claimed that criminals deliberately avoided Delaware because they feared the whipping post;
that once whipped there they promptly left the state; and that as a result, the state had a very low crime rate. The governor of Delaware
maintained that his state did not require a prison because it had retained its whipping post. Savings to the taxpayer from whipping rather
than imprisoning the criminal was an argument occasionally made, although it was not the most important consideration for proponents.

Proponents of the whipping post were more concerned with punishing the wife beater than with aiding or protecting the victim. The
circumstances of the battered wife appeared frequently in argument,
but mostly as an afterthought. They accurately pointed out that criminal punishment of the wife beater had not worked. In most states the

[34] *Report of the Ninth Annual Meeting of the American Bar Association*, p. 291.

[35] U.S., Congress, House, *Congressional Record*, 59th Cong., 1st sess., 1906, 40, pt.
3: 2448.

convicted wife beater was punished by a fine and imprisonment, only to deprive the wife of economic support. Even if her husband was merely fined, the money for the fine came out of the family's funds. Many battered wives refused to complain or dropped their complaints because they could not afford to live without the husband's economic support. Even when wives were willing to help convict their husbands, they soon found themselves unable to support the family, and so they begged judges to release their men from prison. Once the husband returned to work, he began using his wages to buy drink, and when he became drunk, he began to beat his wife.[36]

But while the proponents of the whipping post pointed out serious deficiencies in the punishment of wife beaters, they were unwilling to consider alternatives other than the whipping post. If they had been concerned about encouraging the wife to complain, they could have considered reforming the system of criminal justice. The prosecutor, rather than the wife, could have brought the complaint, so that the burden of pressing charges did not fall on the wife and make her vulnerable to further cruelty from her husband. A court could have ruled it impossible for the victim to drop criminal charges. A trial could have been made mandatory, even when the wife refused to appear in court. A system of work release could have been devised, so that the husband could have served a jail term, while working during the day to support his family.[37]

In England the suffragist Frances Power Cobbe, an opponent of the whipping post, was able to persuade its supporters to favor instead a protection bill for battered wives. Her bill provided a battered wife with a legal separation from her husband, legal custody of her children, and an order requiring her husband to pay her and her children support. Cobbe's bill was passed by Parliament in 1878. She sent a copy of it to the American suffragist Lucy Stone, who introduced a similar bill into the Massachusetts legislature in 1879. Opposition to the bill came from legislators who believed that passage of the law would make it too easy for women to secure legal separation and thus spur dissolution of the family. Stone's bill went down to a resounding defeat. She made

---

[36] "Wife Beaters and their Punishment," *Medico-Legal Journal* 20 (1902–1903): 579.

[37] For an excellent survey of the kinds of remedies with which lawyers and prosecutors are now experimenting see Lisa G. Lerman, "Criminal Prosecution of Wife Beaters," *Response to Violence in the Family* 4, no. 3 (January/February, 1981): 1–19.

two more attempts to pass this bill, but she failed each time. Frustrated by these defeats, Stone, long an opponent of cruel punishments, came to support the whipping post for wife beaters.[38] With even an influential suffragist like Stone favoring the whipping post, pressure on leaders of the campaign to consider other civil or criminal remedies was virtually nil. But the supporters of the whipping post would probably not have been interested in Cobbe's bill. Her remedies made it easier for a wife to gain legal separation and separate maintenance, whereas these men hoped to preserve the family by making the wife beater live up to his manly responsibilities. Cobbe's bill also provided civil remedies for wife beating, whereas these men were interested in strengthening the criminal law.

It was left to the opponents of the whipping post to propose other criminal remedies. The Rev. Antoinette Blackwell believed the wife beater should be sent to prison and put to work there, with his wages going to pay his board in prison and to support his family. She urged that the man remain in prison until he reformed. Quaker prison reformers also backed this remedy; one of them insisted the prison should cure the man of alcoholism before he was released.[39] The Philadelphia Society for Alleviating the Miseries of Public Prisons favored stiffer prison terms for wife beaters convicted a second or third time. But these suggestions were intended to score points in debate, and none of them was implemented.

The most frequent objection of the opponents to the whipping post for wife beaters was that it was a degrading form of punishment, in which a man was treated as a brute. The state was needlessly and with malice causing a man pain. God's law was violated when man was degraded instead of being treated with dignity and respect. The wife beater, suffering disgrace, would become a pariah in his own community, a "wanderer and an outcast on a cold and cheerless world," and only other criminals would accept him.[40] His wife, the innocent victim, would also "meet with a degree of scorn, however undeserved," and

[38] *Documents of the House of Representatives of the Commonwealth of Massachusetts, 1879, House Document No. 14* (Boston: Rand, Avery and Co., 1879); *Woman's Journal*, January 11, 1879.

[39] Blackwell, "Corporal Punishment for Crime," *Medico-Legal Journal* 17, no. 1 (1899): 112. See also *Woman's Journal*, March 31, 1894.

[40] Duane Mowry, "Whipping as a Punishment for Crime: A Reply," *The Green Bag* 12, no. 12 (December, 1901): 555.

even his children would be disgraced. Society would also be degraded. The sole function of society in punishing criminals was to protect itself. Society was permitted to select a punishment that protected itself from repeated crimes, but a whipping went beyond protection to vengeance and retaliation. Civilization had progressed from the days when it relied on barbaric punishments, but it would revert to barbarism if the whipping post was brought back. Even the man who administered the whipping was degraded. Knowledge that criminals were whipped also inflamed the passions of the public and encouraged others, especially impressionable children, in cruelty.

A few opponents also tried to claim that whipping was a "cruel and unusual punishment," prohibited by the U.S. Constitution. But even most of these opponents recognized that the Constitution only prohibited the federal government, not the states, from enacting such statutes. Moreover, the state supreme courts, such as Maryland's, had ruled that whipping was not a cruel and unusual punishment.[41] The opponents concentrated their attack on the whipping post on moral or practical grounds rather than legal ones.

The practical objection was that the whipping post had not deterred crime. Cruel punishment and torture, relied on for thousands of years, had not eliminated the crimes they were intended to punish. Even in the states where flogging had been used, wife beating had not disappeared. Delaware was a small agricultural state that would be relatively free from crime, regardless of what criminal measures it relied on. These opponents were also quite pessimistic about human nature. They believed that men could never be reformed and that the cause of crime was the low level of civilization. Wife beating could never be prevented or even reduced. In the case of wife beaters, there was no effective deterrent. The criminal was an irrational man who never contemplated the punishment he would face for misbehavior. He was a drunkard, a man who beat his wife in a moment of passion.

The opponents also believed that the family would suffer from the flogging of the husband. The man who was flogged would take out his anger on his family.[42] He would treat them the way he had been treated. (They, too, assumed that he would return home, at least tem-

[41] "Whipping Not a Cruel and Unusual Punishment," *Criminal Law Magazine* 4, no. 3 (May, 1883): 401–10; see also Charles Foote v. State of Maryland, 59 Md. 264 (1882).
[42] *Woman's Journal*, February 11, 1905, March 11, 1905, and February 3, 1906.

porarily, if only to punish his family. Other opponents, however, claimed that the flogged man would desert his family rather than seeing the disgrace he suffered in their eyes.) The family suffered in other ways. The wife beater would be so degraded in the eyes of employers that he could not find a job. One Maryland husband who had been whipped had to appeal to the attorney general of the state for a letter persuading employers to hire him.[43] It would be comforting if one could show that those concerned about the plight of the injured wife were women or suffragists. But in fact suffragist opinion was about equally divided: Stone did not believe that the wife would suffer greater danger from a husband who had been whipped, but among those who expressed the most concern for the safety of the battered wife were police chiefs and judges.

While most of the arguments against the whipping post were serious ones, some of the opponents considered wife beating a joking matter. Their most effective weapon was ridicule. When a whipping post bill was being debated in Delaware, one opponent introduced a bill to punish wives who beat their husbands. His bill never came to a vote.[44] At the annual meeting of the American Bar Association the issue was taken seriously until one lawyer rose to wonder how the wife who beat her husband would be punished. Then taking up the mood of jocularity, another lawyer wanted to amend the resolution by adding "that any one convicted of the crime of rape should be burned at the stake."[45] In congressional debate, members of the U.S. Congress were concerned that a husband had been provoked by a coy damsel "weighing about 300 pounds, with auburn hair."[46] What were the circumstances in which wife beating occurred? It was not a brutal assault by a drunken husband on a Saturday night, as proponents claimed, but a good laboring man, not a drunkard at all, who came home at night to find his wife had not cooked supper. The wife was a nag, "a woman that has a tongue with a sharp edge on each side and as rough as a file on its bottom, which she constantly uses from morning until night."[47] These men were simply reviving the popular stereotype of the battered

[43] *Medico-Legal Journal* 17, no. 1 (1899): 100.

[44] Caldwell, *Red Hannah*, p. 35.

[45] *Report of the Tenth Annual Meeting of the American Bar Association*, p. 78.

[46] U.S., Congress, House, *Congressional Record*, 59th Cong., 1st sess., 1906, pt. 3: 2448.

[47] Ibid., p. 2450.

woman as a shrew who provoked her husband into beating her. They used ridicule to discredit the idea that wife beating was a serious issue, and they sought to attack the view that the victim was innocent and helpless. They helped to destroy the possibility of serious consideration for any options to the whipping post for wife beaters.

The last success of the campaign to punish wife beating with the whipping post came in 1905. The Oregon law punished wife beating with a whipping, a fine, or a prison term.[48] Perhaps President Theodore Roosevelt deserves credit for this victory. In his fourth annual message to Congress in 1904, he decried "brutality and cruelty towards the weak." Roosevelt wrote, "The wifebeater, for example, is inadequately punished by imprisonment; for imprisonment may often mean nothing to him, while it may cause hunger and want to the wife and children who have been the victims of his brutality. Probably some form of corporal punishment would be the most adequate way of meeting this crime."[49] As governor of New York, Roosevelt had first gone on record in favor of the whipping post for wife beaters. He was a personal friend of Simeon Baldwin, Clark Bell, and Robert Adams, and he had long favored other reforms to protect the weak and defenseless. But while Roosevelt's popularity may have carried the day in Oregon, he did not sway the U.S. House of Representatives. In fact, some congressional opponents insisted that inasmuch as Roosevelt had simply called for some form of corporal punishment, he had not actually favored the whipping post.

But semantics aside, this was an issue whose time had come and gone. The largest number of whippings for wife beating in Delaware were administered in the early years of the twentieth century—1906 was the high point—and thereafter the flogging of wife beaters declined. Delaware reformers even scored a partial victory when the state's legislature abolished the pillory in 1905, although the whipping post was retained. By 1913 a Montana congressman introduced legislation in the House of Representatives to abolish Delaware's whipping post. He argued that the whipping was a cruel and unusual punishment prohibited by the federal Constitution, and he requested that

[48] State of Oregon, *The General Laws, 1905* (Salem, Ore.: J. R. Whitney, 1905), pp. 335–36.

[49] Fred L. Israel, ed., *The State of the Union: Messsages of the Presidents, 1790–1966*, vol. 2 (New York: Chelsea House, 1977), p. 2116.

the U.S. attorney general prevent Delaware officials from administering whippings. The attorney general decided that the federal courts did not have the power to issue an injunction, and that Delaware was free to use the lash without federal interference. This decision stilled the congressional debate about Delaware's whipping post.

But nothing could still old firehorses like Clark Bell. As late as 1913 he was still denouncing "the mock humanitarians of our age. . . . Give me a Delaware whipping post in New York City," he requested of the readers of the *Medico-Legal* journal, "and I will eliminate wife-beating in that city or any other American city."[50] One magistrate in New York began to advocate the whipping post for husbands who deserted their wives.[51] But between 1911 and 1917 the movement to end capital punishment was renewed. Newspapers that once called for a return to the whipping post now denounced it as "uncivilized" and a grotesque anachronism. By 1925 a warden of the Delaware state prison was explaining, "We haven't had a wifebeater for years." Whenever a whipping was administered, he said, he received a flood of letters of protest from all parts of the country.[52] The whipping post was abolished in Maryland in 1948 and in Delaware in 1952.

After the demise of this campaign, there was to be no public effort on behalf of battered wives for another seventy years. But it is unlikely that there would have been more public interest in the intervening years, even if wife beating had not become associated with punitive attitudes toward criminals. In England, where Frances Power Cobbe diverted the flogging campaign in a more humanitarian direction, interest in the issue of wife beating still waned by the turn of the century. In the United States, by the time public attitudes toward criminals had turned more conservative, wife beating had become firmly ensconced as a family problem or a symptom of mental illness. It was no longer a criminal matter that could generate a moral crusade.

In all of human history, there have been only a few short epochs when the public was forced to consider wife beating as a serious matter of social policy. We are living through one of them. But in our own time, wife beating is defined as an issue of interest mainly to women, a

[50] Bell, "The Cat as a Deterrent for Crime," p. 946.
[51] R. W. Shufeldt, "The Whipping Post for Wife Beaters," *The Arena* 35, no. 194 (January, 1906): 168–71.
[52] Caldwell, *Red Hannah*, p. 49.

topic of concern raised by the women's movement, which has valiantly tried to persuade police chiefs, judges, and district attorneys to enforce the law against wife beaters. In the late nineteenth century, law enforcement officials on their own initiative not only regarded wife beating as a serious crime but financed and led a campaign to punish the criminals. Wealthy, highly conservative, powerful men publicly proclaimed their sympathy for the suffering of women and insisted that in virtually all cases of wife beating, right was on the woman's side. They recognized that the criminal law had to be used to protect women victims. A U.S. president even denounced wife beating in his annual message to Congress and called for the enforcement of the law against wife beaters.

Despite the prestige, power, and influence of the leaders and supporters of this campaign, it failed to achieve its legislative goal. We should be grateful that the campaign never tried to arouse the public in support of this legislation because the emotions generated could have been easily used to stir repression. In the states in which the whipping post was erected, it quickly became a dead letter. But when the cat was used, it was disproportionately black men who were flogged. The fact that the whipping post laws could not be enforced was even used as an argument against the enforcement of any criminal laws against wife beaters. Whipping was claimed to be the only punishment for wife beating that was severe enough. But wives in Maryland and Delaware had not wanted their husbands whipped. Therefore, the criminal law had tried the one penalty that could work, but temerity of battered wives had doomed it to defeat. No further efforts were needed.

There was more to be feared had the campaign succeeded. The proponents were ready to campaign for the castration of rapists and the flogging of juvenile criminals. It is also unlikely that the whipping post would have ensured the equal treatment of women, as its proponents claimed. The criminal law would probably have been used against women, at least the "impure" ones, as well as to protect those who were innocent. The leaders of the campaign claimed that a strengthened criminal law would undercut the appeal of vigilantes. But one could easily imagine that lynch mobs would have been encouraged by these punitive measures and would have demanded even harsher ones, without the impediment of lawyers and jury trials. Extreme repression could easily have degenerated into lawlessness.

The proponents of the whipping post were more menacing than its opponents, although neither side deserves unqualified praise or condemnation. In this debate both sides largely neglected the question of how best to aid and protect women victims. All were prisoners of heavy-handed Victorian rhetoric about drunken brutes and their helpless victims. Advocates of the whipping post were concerned about the right issue, but mostly for the wrong reasons. Opponents were not as concerned about the issue—some of them even considered it a joke—although they were right in opposing the whipping post on humanitarian grounds. They failed, however, in adequately developing or implementing policies other than punishment at the whipping post. Stone deserves credit for posing the only serious suffragist alternative in the United States. Should we then excuse or simply avoid in embarrassment her support of the whipping post for wife beaters?

When the highly emotional issue of wife beating was joined with the demand for the flogging of criminals, it functioned to bolster the claims of those who urged increased criminal penalties and greater power for judges and police in handling criminals. The sufferings of women were recited to help law enforcement officials gain control over dangerous criminals. Can one define wife beating as a crime without strengthening the hand of those who want to arm the state against the lower classes, the young, and the black? There is great reason to feel pessimistic, generally cautious, and even a little sad that so much heat generated so little light.

Contributors

DAVID LEVINE teaches history and the history of education at the Ontario Institute for Studies in Education. He is the author of *Family Formation in an Age of Nascent Capitalism* and *Poverty and Piety in an English Village: Terling, 1525–1700* (with Keith Wrightson). He is currently at work with Keith Wrightson on a study of the social history and demography of coal miners.

LESLIE PAGE MOCH is assistant professor of history at the University of Texas at Arlington. She is the author of *Paths to the City: Regional Migration in Nineteenth-Century France*. She is beginning a study of the village schoolteacher and the implementation of educational policy in Republican France, 1880–1914.

JOHN MODELL is professor of history at Carnegie-Mellon University. His books include *The Economics and Politics of Racial Accommodation: The Japanese of Los Angeles 1900–1942* and *The Economic Basis of Ethnic Solidarity: Small Business in the Japanese American Community* (with Edna Bonacich). He is engaged in a study of family formation in twentieth-century America.

ELIZABETH H. PLECK is a research associate with the Wellesley College Center for Research on Women. Her books include *Black Migration and Poverty: Boston, 1865–1900*, *The American Man* (with Joseph Pleck), and *A Heritage of Her Own: Toward a New History of American Women* (with Nancy Cott). She is currently at work on a history of domestic violence in the United States.

LOUISE A. TILLY teaches history at the University of Michigan. Her books published in English are *The Rebellious Century* (with Charles Tilly and Richard Tilly), *Women, Work and Family* (with Joan Scott), and *Class Conflict and Collective Action* (with Charles Tilly). Her current work includes *The Formation of a Working Class: Milan, 1880–1900*. Louise Tilly is president of the Social Science History Association.